Fantasy \ făn´tə-sē : the free play of the imagination; creative thinking or subconscious mental activity that may distort, enhance, or otherwise affect perceptions or what a person produces. Fantasy is not limited by conscious, wakeful, or rational reasoning. It acts or functions in the abstract realm of ideas. Desire, fear, history, or intellectual pursuit may drive fantasy, but, whatever its motivation or content, fantasy is not palpable; it is not knowable in a physical sense. Fantasy or its adjectival form, fantastical, may be used to describe novels, movies, artworks, or experiences, but to apply these words as descriptions is not equal to fully revealing the nature of fantasy, which is inherently ineffable, purely conceptual, and located in discourse.

Underfoot \ ŭn′dər-fŏŏt′: under the foot and against the ground. Underfoot refers directly to an actual location and is readily distinguished from vague notions of place such as "the world of ideas" or "in discourse." Underfoot does not denote a conceptual meaning. When something is underfoot, it is, for example, between the fleshy underside of a foot and what supports it, such as dense grass or a cement sidewalk. One feels what is underfoot, tickling, irritating, sticking, pressing, or poking and potentially injurious. To consider this base locale, or the experience of an item positioned there, is not a lofty affair. Rather, it is mundane. Unlike fantasy, underfoot suggests something knowable in a physical sense.

The 47th Corcoran Biennial
fantasy underfoot

Washington, D.C.   Corcoran Gallery of Art   2002

The 47th Corcoran Biennial

fantasy underfoot

Jonathan P. Binstock

Foreword by
Jacquelyn Days Serwer

with essays by
Matthew Biro
Billy Collins
Adam Lerner
Stacey Schmidt

Published on the occasion of the exhibition *The 47th Corcoran Biennial: Fantasy Underfoot*, organized by the Corcoran Gallery of Art, Washington, D.C., on view from December 21, 2002, to March 10, 2003.

Curator: Jonathan P. Binstock
Assistant Curator: Stacey Schmidt
Editor: Janet Wilson
Catalogue Design: Robert Villaflor
Exhibition Design: Linda McNamara Rice
    for Quatrefoil Associates
Printing: Kelly Press, Cheverly, Md.

The 47th Corcoran Biennial: Fantasy Underfoot is sponsored by The Broad Art Foundation, the FRIENDS of the Corcoran, the Anna E. Clark Fund, Anne and Ronald Abramson, Ellen and Gerry Sigal, the Canadian Embassy, Jon and NoraLee Sedmak, the Elizabeth Firestone Graham Foundation, the William A. Clark Awards, and The President's Exhibition Fund.

ISBN 0-88675-069-5
ISSN 8756-4777

cover: Nancy Davidson, *Study #1 for Double Exposure*, 2002, photomontage, 10 1/8 x 13". Courtesy the artist and Robert Miller Gallery, New York

frontispiece: Janet Cardiff and George Bures Miller, exterior view of *The Paradise Institute*, 2001. Courtesy Luhring Augustine, New York, and Galerie Barbara Weiss, Berlin; view of installation at Hamburger Bahnhof, Berlin

foreword: Jacob El Hanani, *Basket (from the "Basket" series)*(detail), 2002. Courtesy Nicole Klagsbrun Gallery, New York

CONTENTS

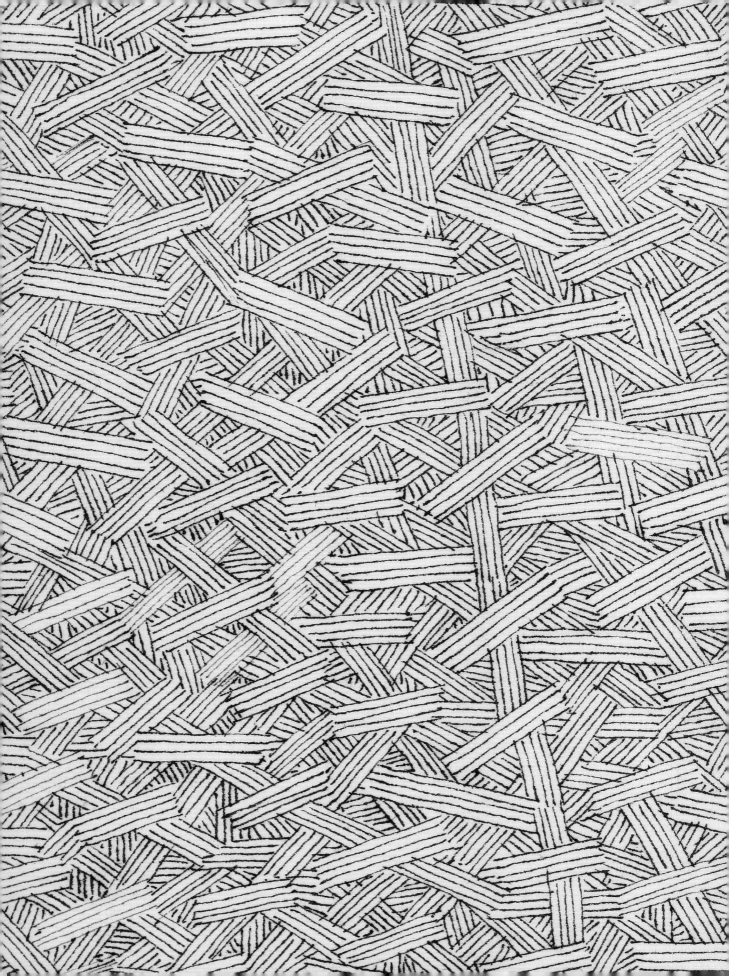

The 47th Corcoran Biennial

The 47th Corcoran Biennial marks ninety-five years since the inaugural exhibition in 1907. For over nine decades, the Biennial has celebrated contemporary art in America and made it accessible to a broad audience. The first Biennial attracted almost 63,000 visitors (at a time when Washington, D.C.'s population was about 300,000) over the course of a month, demonstrating the public's keen interest in the art of the time. Until the founding of the Hirshhorn Museum and Sculpture Garden in 1974, the Corcoran Biennial was the only opportunity for museumgoers in the nation's capital to see a major presentation of contemporary art.

Over the past century, the Biennial evolved from a survey of contemporary trends in American painting to a more personal selection largely decided by a single curator. Through 1967, the Biennials featured two categories of paintings, one by invited artists and the other selected by a jury from submitted works. Since then, all of the artists chosen for the Biennial have been invited and are usually represented by works that relate to a unifying theme. In the 1970s director Walter Hopps favored abstract art; in the 1980s guest curator Lisa Lyons and curator of contemporary art Ned Rifkin organized exhibi-tions with a regional focus. Since the early 1990s, the exhibition has featured artists in small solo shows of recent work or work created especially for the Biennial.

In all its phases, the Biennial has played a major role in the Corcoran's exhibition program, fulfilling its mission to educate and serve the public and promoting the growth of the Museum's permanent collection. In the 7th (1919) and 9th (1923) Biennials, for example, the Ashcan paintings of Robert Henri—which demonstrated the Corcoran's acceptance of new subject matter—were juxtaposed with the works of Frederick Frieseke and Cecilia Beaux, artists still grounded in nineteenth-cen-tury impressionist traditions. This amounted to a some-what delayed recognition of dramatic changes in the American art world, but one that caused the Corcoran's audience of art lovers to take note.

During the latter half of the twentieth century, Biennial artists tended to reflect the more daring end of the contemporary art spectrum. Lee Bontecou and Jimmy Ernst starred in the 28th Biennial (1963), and Gene Davis, Paul Jenkins, and Jules Olitski headlined the 30th Biennial (1967). By the 43rd Biennial (1993), the challenging and disturbing images of Ida Applebroog,

Kim Dingle, and Charles Garabedian set a new standard for contemporary painters working in the representational sphere. Jessica Stockholder, in the 44th Biennial (1995), demonstrated the prerogative of younger artists to ignore the boundaries between painting and other media. In her signature piece, *1994*, fabric, found objects, and papier-mâché combine to create a colorful ensemble that moved painting into the realm of sculpture and installation art.

The Biennial has not only ensured a dialogue between the Corcoran's audience and the world of working artists but, from the first, has also served an essential function in the Museum's acquisitions program. More than one-fifth of the American paintings in the permanent collection have come from the Biennials, either as direct Museum purchases from the exhibitions or as gifts from collectors who had bought Biennial works.

In 1998 the Corcoran's 45th Biennial paid homage to almost a century of these exhibitions. The scholarly catalogue and exhibition of works selected from past Biennials helped to recapture the story of the Corcoran's aggressive role in showcasing and collecting contemporary art. During the exhibition visitors were invited to vote on their favorite work, a regular procedure in the early years. John Singer Sargent's *Simplon Pass* (1911), one of the museum's most valued possessions from the early twentieth century, emerged as the all-time crowd pleaser.

The 45th Biennial signaled the end of an era. After many decades of showcasing American painting, the Museum decided to expand the boundaries of the subsequent Biennial to include other media and artists of different nationalities. Although painting remains an active and viable medium, many artists have extended their sphere of creativity to include photography or photo-based media, video, film, and computers, as well as installation and performance art. It also seemed an arbitrary practice to automatically exclude artists of other nationalities, particularly those working in America.

The 46th Biennial in 2000, *Media/Metaphor*, explored the dissolution of traditional aesthetic and philosophical barriers, which has inspired artists to use new technologies for expressive ends. The exhibition fostered a dialogue that emphasized the easy give-and-take between art forms. Painters David Reed, Lisa Yuskavage, and Ben Sakoguchi shared similar concerns about issues of representation, narrative, and illusion, as did Shimon Attie in his photographs and videos, Y. David Chung in his computer-enhanced animated videos, and Chuck Close in his recent daguerreotypes. Even the high-tech team of Jennifer Steinkamp and Jimmy Johnson, represented by *Loop,* a computer-generated light and sound environment, considered the ways in which color and scale determine the visitor's experience.

Fantasy Underfoot, the 47th Biennial, continues this more expansive approach to the selection of artists and media. It includes the versatile Bruce Nauman, who presents a new video work derived from nighttime observations of his deserted studio; Janet Cardiff and George Bures Miller, the Canadian team of video and sound artists, whose work unfolds in a self-contained theater; computer whiz Ken Feingold, father to a family of animatronic mannequins; and sculptors Tim Hawkinson and Nancy Davidson. Hawkinson and Davidson are both known for employing oversized inflatable materials. Hawkinson uses sound as well as sight to create his illusions, while Davidson relies on the startling effect of massive forms that suggest female breasts or buttocks floating in the air, dispelling any conventional notions of body or gravity.

The female anatomy also plays a central role in Susan Smith-Pinelo's work. Videos featuring full-frame shots of the most evocative body parts bouncing to rousing hip-hop tunes create an irrepressible urge to crash the party. The romance of Smith-Pinelo's pop music, like the romance of Bruce Yonemoto's nostalgic video interpretations of old movies and Nigel Poor's portraits of personal objects, transports the viewer to the land of lost loves and second chances.

Many of the artists introduce us to larger worlds unencumbered by reality, but Marcel Dzama and Jacob El Hanani create detailed drawings—narrative and abstract, respectively—that draw us irresistibly into miniature universes, like that of Alice down the rabbit hole.

Painters Linda Besemer and Kojo Griffin maintain the Biennial's commitment to a more traditional medium. Besemer's abstract compositions, independent of any canvas or other kind of support, bear no physical resemblance to Griffin's haunting images. However, these painters, as well as the other artists in the exhibition, have something in common. They all strive to lift us out of our ordinary experience into a realm that will nourish our imagination and enrich our understanding of both the real and the illusory worlds revealed in their work.

The Corcoran has come a long way from the galleries of traditional paintings in its early Biennials. By responding to the new, more complex world of media-savvy artists, the Corcoran continues its commitment to presenting examples of the most exciting art being produced today. *Fantasy Underfoot* offers an exhilarating exploration of artworks that are as intriguing as they are fresh and unpredictable.

In addition to the artists participating in the exhibition and the art historians who have written for the catalogue, we are especially indebted to Billy Collins, poet laureate of the United States, 2001–2003, for his illuminating contribution to this publication. As only a poet can do, he has managed in a very few words to summon the spirit of our latest Biennial enterprise. His insights on the theme and the parallels between the task of the poet and that of the visual artist help us to better comprehend and appreciate both endeavors while reminding us of why they mean so much.

Jacquelyn Days Serwer
Chief Curator

LENDERS TO THE EXHIBITION

Ace Gallery, Los Angeles

Angles Gallery, Santa Monica, Calif.

The Artists

Blum & Poe, Santa Monica, Calif.

Leslie Camhi, New York

Fusebox, Washington, D.C.

Gallery Joe, Philadelphia

Haines Gallery, San Francisco

Mr. and Mrs. Frank Herringer

Anne Hoger and Robert Conn, Del Mar, Calif.

Nicole Klagsbrun, New York

Nicole Klagsbrun Gallery, New York

Phyllis and John Kleinberg

lemon sky: projects + editions, Los Angeles

Curtis Liberda and Chris Esworthy, Dallas

Luhring Augustine, New York

P. Bruce Marine and Donald Hardy Collection

Robert Miller Gallery, New York

Mitchell-Innes & Nash, New York

Postmasters Gallery, New York

Private Collections

Saltworks Gallery, Atlanta

Sperone Westwater Gallery, New York

Walker Art Center, Minneapolis

David Zwirner, New York

PREFACE AND ACKNOWLEDGMENTS

When I arrived at the Corcoran in January 2001 as the new curator of contemporary art, *The 46th Corcoran Biennial: Media/Metaphor* had just opened. Like almost everyone connected with the Corcoran, I was very proud of the exhibition, enjoying the excitement and success of what was proving to be a defining moment in the institution's history. *Media/Metaphor* was the first in the long-standing series of Biennial exhibitions to transcend the media-defined boundary of painting. With its video projections, installations, and photographs, the exhibition signaled a new era. The door was now wide open for future Biennials to feature art in virtually any form. I immediately started thinking about the possibilities for the next effort.

Surveying the national scene with an awareness of what was happening in Europe and the rest of the world, I noted a trend, particularly evident since the 1990s, that I would later describe as the "conceptual vernacular." The phrase refers to art that seems to be conceptually driven yet is user-friendly and, moreover, emphasizes this usually incompatible combination. I did not know at the time that curator Richard Francis had already used these same words in 1994 in an exhibition

he organized for the Museum of Contemporary Art in Chicago. However, Francis uses the term to refer to postmodern theory and nonhierarchical approaches to subject matter, while I construe it more generally, as the overt representation of ideas in standard, common, or familiar forms. For this reason the term, though the same as Francis's, has new relevance in the context of this project, the 47th Corcoran Biennial.

The idea of the conceptual vernacular would eventually lead me to explore a group of issues that extend beyond art, including contemporary museology. As I amassed a list of artists and works that seemed to be consistent with my perceptions of this major trend, I was guided only by my intellectual and instinctual responses to the experience of viewing, and not by an array of requirements. I narrowed the candidates by making many difficult decisions based on determinations of quality and a desire to include a cross-section of forms, media, and generations of artists. Unlike some Biennials, which strive to be inclusive, this one represents a slice of contemporary practice that includes only thirteen artists. Nonetheless, it points to an important and far-reaching aspect of contemporary production that continues to grow. The resulting exhibition is an experiment. It seeks to embody the sense of immediacy, comprehensibility, and also the intellectual abstractness inherent in the featured works.

Despite my belief in the link between the art, arriving at a language to describe this was a great challenge. The following essay is an effort to take stock of my research, findings, and final decisions. The ideas presented are most accurately understood as the outcome, rather than the premise, of the exhibition. The essay explores some thoughts and feelings that many viewers may develop on their own as they reflect on the installation.

This publication contains fifteen other essays that offer, in creative and productive ways, diverse angles on the issues raised by this Biennial, ranging from contributions by Adam Lerner and U.S. Poet Laureate Billy Collins, which address the overarching themes of the project, to those devoted to specific artists and their work. During the course of my research, Lerner's sharp insights and thoughtful comments enhanced my observations of the current art scene. These conversations ultimately led to his essay in this volume. I am grateful for our discourse, and especially for his scholarly contribution, which brings a museological perspective to the project.

In his essay "The Poetry Shuttle," Billy Collins demonstrates the rare talent of being able to write on the subject of transcendence through art while offering the possibility of such transcendence through his poetic prose. In thinking about the conceptual vernacular, I realized that there is something of a parallel effect in Collins's poems, which have the uncanny ability to take us from the here and now, the concrete, to "the indeterminate," to borrow his words. I am very grateful for his willingness to participate in this project by contributing an essay and one of his recent poems, "Study in Orange and White," which is particularly relevant to the exhibition.

In addition to Lerner, Matthew Biro and Stacey Schmidt wrote informative essays on the individual artists. Working with Biro provided the added pleasure of employing one of the professors who sat on my dissertation committee, a turning of the tables that resulted in two excellent essays on Ken Feingold and Tim Hawkinson. Stacey Schmidt, the Corcoran's assistant curator of contemporary art, tackled the bulk of the artist-

specific writings, producing six fine essays that merit my deep appreciation. I would also like to thank Jacquelyn Days Serwer, chief curator of the Museum. In addition to writing the ideal foreword, which places the present Biennial in its proper institutional and historical contexts, she has supported my aspirations from the start when they were the mere glimmer of an idea. I am most grateful for her continued belief in me and in this project.

Alan Wallach, Ralph H. Wark Professor of Art and Art History and professor of American studies at the College of William and Mary, a renowned specialist in the study of museum history and practice, kindly reviewed the overarching essays by Lerner and myself. He was an astute critic who provided an excellent sounding board for our ideas. Maurice Berger, senior fellow, Vera List Center for Art and Politics, New School University, who is both a friend and a colleague, read and criticized my thematic essay. His comments were most perceptive and much appreciated. I am also grateful to Angela Westwater, whose observations about Bruce Nauman's art were helpful as I wrote the essay devoted to his most recent series of video installations.

Neither the catalogue nor the exhibition would have been possible without the generous consideration of foundations, institutions, individuals, and friends who have loaned art to the exhibition, for which I am most grateful, or provided support in other important ways. The following have graciously underwritten this project, and all of them have my sincere gratitude: The Broad Art Foundation, the FRIENDS of the Corcoran, Anne and Ronald Abramson, Ellen and Gerry Sigal, the Canadian Embassy, Jon and NoraLee Sedmak, the Elizabeth Firestone Graham Foundation, and The President's Exhibition Fund. For their efforts in securing sponsorship, I would also like to express my appreciation to Katy Ahmed, director of corporate relations and events; Kate Gibney, director of foundation relations; Donna Stubbs, corporate relations and events specialist; and Deborah Mueller, development associate.

A number of individuals outside the Corcoran were helpful well beyond the call of duty in the planning and organization of this project, and their assistance is gratefully acknowledged: Lilli Andresen and Tim Christian of Angles Gallery, Santa Monica, Calif.;

Claudia Altman-Siegel of Luhring Augustine, New York; Carlo Cravato; Bellatrix Hubert and Eugenia Lai of David Zwirner, New York; Bruce Hackney of Nicole Klagsbrun Gallery, New York; Leta Grzan of Mitchell-Innes & Nash, New York; Michael Short of Sperone Westwater Gallery, New York; John Bowsher, exhibitions director at the Dia Art Foundation; Bryan Jackson; James Huckenphaler; and Brian Miller of Core, a design firm in Washington, D.C. I would also like to thank Ann Movalson, who offered her support in many ways, including as a vital respondent to some of my most fledgling ideas.

Biennial exhibitions are a peculiar type of project. The moment one is completed, another is begun, and two years is a less than ideal amount of time to organize a major exhibition and produce an accompanying catalogue. Despite this challenging schedule, everyone at the Corcoran involved with the project met its demands with extraordinary talent, efficiency, and grace. Elizabeth Parr, exhibitions director, handled the many complex details related to coordinating the exhibition. Without her experience, ingenuity, and patience, this project would have been difficult to realize. Other Museum staff members who executed their responsibilities with diligent professionalism and who merit special thanks are Susan Badder, senior curator of education; Kimberly Davis, registrar; Ken Ashton, museum technician; Clyde Paton, preparator; David Jung, assistant preparator; and Chris Williams and Corey Hixson, art handlers. Robert Villaflor designed this handsome catalogue, and Janet Wilson edited the manuscript in her usual fashion, with a dependably keen eye and intellect. The interns who assisted in indispensable ways were Kelly Ditto, Mary Hendrickse, Kate Werble, and Conner Williams.

Behind the art are the support structures on which it rests and the building in which it is housed. Because the Corcoran is a very old building, the task of creating a fitting environment for the logistically challenging works in this exhibition—some of which presented tricky new demands on the existing architecture—was exceptionally difficult. Steve Brown, senior director of operations; Mike McCullough, construction manager; Annie Wilson, audiovisual technician; and Abby Frankson, lighting specialist, were up to this task in ways that made solving the many problems seem easy. Linda

McNamara Rice of Quatrefoil Design produced the elegant and practical designs for the exhibition spaces.

Finally, I would like to thank David C. Levy, the Corcoran's president and director, and Michael Roark, chief financial and administrative officer. While my colleagues and I were attending to the daily concerns of organizing the Biennial, they were running the institution with a deep appreciation for contemporary art and, in particular, the tradition of the Corcoran Biennial. Their support has been invaluable.

Jonathan P. Binstock
Curator of Contemporary Art

Fantasy Underfoot

Jonathan P. Binstock, Curator of Contemporary Art, Corcoran Gallery of Art

Visual art since the nineteenth century may be characterized as a conceptual gesture that takes the form of a concrete object or image. Whether a painting or a photograph, an installation or a video, all art begins as an idea and is born of intellectual labor. The starting point is typically a question; for example, an artist may ask, What will I make, or how will I make it? If the question is tackled and art is made, the intangible thought evolves into a material thing, which ultimately takes its place among all the other things that constitute the world. We may distinguish art objects from other kinds of objects for any number of reasons, ranging from their appearance—a very old strategy for determining what art is—to how they relate to the context in which they are presented; this modern strategy was first articulated in 1913 by Marcel Duchamp, who recontextualized ordinary objects and called them readymade artworks. In either case, whether referring to the production, appearance, or interpretation of an artwork, it can never be disassociated from the abstract ideas and discourse that inform its existence as art.

The inspiration for *The 47th Corcoran Biennial: Fantasy Underfoot* emanates from the relationship between concepts and concrete objects that characterizes art of the modern era. A vast topic, to be sure, the dynamic of this relationship has changed dramatically since the mid-1960s, when the subject was urgently debated in and around the practice of conceptual art and the "new media" of film and video. These historical debates and the art that gave rise to them contributed to an important shift in the kind of work some artists make and the way art institutions exhibit it. *Fantasy Underfoot* explores the legacy of conceptual art and the new media of the late sixties through the work of thirteen contemporary artists for whom ideas are, in a sense, a plastic medium.

The artists in *Fantasy Underfoot* were selected because of the impact of their work and the ways they resolve complex theoretical issues using what might be called a conceptual vernacular.[1] Their videos, films, photography, paintings, drawings, sculpture, installations, and digital works all employ familiar or readily understood forms designed to quickly seduce and engage the viewer. The result is an exhibition that promotes a sense of immediacy and comprehensibility while offering an intellectual exercise that operates on a number of levels. This Biennial exhibition takes stock of a dominant trend in recent art that exploits familiar or appealing forms, many of which derive from the mass media, for overtly conceptual ends. *Fantasy Underfoot*, a resonant metaphor to encourage further understanding of these strategies of engagement, suggests that deeper realms of consciousness are close at hand, that fantasy, fantastical revelation, and the abstract world of ideas are concrete matters in the realm of art.

The notion that works of art are essentially composed of two elements, concepts and objects, is as old as Duchamp's readymades, but it was most fully explored during the conceptual art movement, whose heyday lasted roughly from 1966 to 1972.[2] Conceptual artists generally sought to distinguish the paramount ideas that inform the basis of art from perceptual encounters and the often-valuable objects to which art has been traditionally linked. The stereotypical conceptualist tended to turn a given exhibition space into a study center, with placards posted and bound pages arrayed on tabletops, entreating the infrequent visitor to concentrate intensively on the usually dry, esoteric material on display. Despite their primary interest in ideas and discourse, conceptualists were, ironically, often motivated by material concerns, in particular the hope of producing certain societal effects. Conceptual art was in large part a social movement, not unlike others of the late 1960s, that questioned authority and sought to renegotiate the individual's relationship to the larger social order.[3] By ridding their work of obvious aesthetic content and making it difficult to sell, conceptual artists believed they were wresting art from the control of powerful institutions such as museums and the commercial art market. They were acting on the belief, political in nature, that art should not be yet another means by which the rich and powerful could exploit "the system" and further strengthen their authority.

An especially memorable conceptual art moment occurred in 1969, when Robert Barry inaugurated his exhibition at the Art & Project Gallery in Amsterdam by hanging a sign on the front door that stated, "During the exhibition the gallery will be closed" (fig. 1). Barry's closed-gallery project is perhaps the most famous instance of what critics Lucy Lippard and John Chandler described in 1968 as "dematerialized art."[4] Not only was there no art to see, there was also no accessible exhibition space in which to gather and discuss the absence of the work. Barry's art was to shut down an establishment where art is normally viewed and sold. Here was an example of conceptualism that was virtually all concept and no object.

There was something heady and exceedingly intellectual about the best conceptual work of this era. In many ways it was the logical outgrowth of the discursive tactic

fig. 1 Robert Barry, *Closed Gallery Piece*, 1969, three gallery invitations, printed ink on paper, 5 1/8 x 7 1/8, 5 1/2 x 5 1/2, and 11 5/8 x 16 1/2". Courtesy Gasser and Grunert Inc., New York. Barry's closed-gallery project had three parts, as it took place in three galleries: Art & Project Gallery, Amsterdam; Galeria Sperone, Turin, Italy; and Eugenia Butler Gallery, Los Angeles. Pictured here are the notices for each segment of the project.

invoked by minimalism, the immediately preceding art movement. Like conceptual art, minimalism seemed to beg for discourse and, notoriously, for academic jargon to explain its significance. Consider, for example, the precise geometry and pristine surfaces of Donald Judd's industrially fabricated sculptures or the lean configuration of Tony Smith's work: such reticence toward expression appeared likely to deflect interpretive efforts (fig. 2). It comes as no surprise that work with such minimal formal attributes was well suited to theory. These interpretations were destined to be read and appreciated by a very small subset of art professionals. Sometimes the critics were the artists themselves, explaining their work and contributing to a history as rooted in literature as in the art itself. In retrospect, it is clear that minimalism signaled the disassociation of ideas from objects that would later characterize conceptual art. Minimalism was yoked to austere and challenging aesthetic works. Conceptual art, particularly the type that approached a dematerialized state such as Barry's, had almost no physical basis. It existed entirely in the mind, that is, in discourse, in language.

The sign that Barry hung on the door of the Art & Project Gallery was not an art object per se, but rather a suggestion that something connected with artistic practice was afoot. This was particularly the case for those who knew of Barry's intention to hang the sign. For those who were unaware of Barry's clever gesture but were planning to visit the gallery, the paradoxical sign would at least have been a curious indication that something out of the ordinary was taking place. Or it might have been completely perplexing. Either way, the sign and the situation would have called for further contemplation. And for those who were entirely unaware of Barry's enterprise, those who did not care about the information it conveyed or who read it mistakenly, the gallery was simply closed. Any passerby might have discovered as much.

What is important to note here is that this last group of people, indifferent to and disengaged from the gist of the piece, were no more distanced from the artist's intended audience than the well-informed group who

fig. 2 Tony Smith, *Cigarette*, mild steel, vaporized surface, 15 3/4 x 14 7/8 x 14 3/4". Museum Purchase, William A. Clark Fund

knew that the sign was evidence of art. In effect, Barry's project was without limitations. Its central text, the sign, was meant to restrict points of view and close down options for discussion. In the end, it had an opposite result, substantially increasing the project's audience.[5] In effect, the entire street became Barry's palette.

Commentators rarely take the democratic angle in discussing conceptual art, but it was central to a lot of the work. A number of artists chose language precisely because it could blend seamlessly into the discourse of the broader culture and reach a wider audience, one not necessarily linked to the art world.[6] For example, in 1968 Dan Graham published artworks in *Harper's Bazaar* in the guise of advertisements with captions, advertising being a language that anyone could understand (fig. 3). There were no prerequisites, nor was special knowledge required, to be a member of Graham's or Barry's target audience. It was inevitable and desirable that different people would experience the projects in different ways and understand them on different levels. Artists have long desired larger audiences for their work. It seems ironic that some conceptualists found a way— through their art's underlying democratic character— to participate in this effort, considering the limited audience that sustained their art and, even today, continues to propagate its memory.

A given work of art may be difficult to grasp in its entirety, but it may nonetheless speak to many different

fig. 3 Dan Graham, *Figurative by Dan Graham*, 1968. *Harper's Bazaar* (March 1968): 90

Hollywood makes movies.[8] Characters on the screen sometimes sound as if they are in the audience sitting right next to you. Or is it that you, the viewer, are somehow the film's protagonist, and maybe the villain's next victim? The cinematic context suggests something familiar, but the feeling of being caught in between fiction and real-time, real-world experience is not. Although it may be difficult to determine what a given viewer will take away from this piece, one can predict that he or she, with headphones on, will be immersed in its representation of an entirely new narrative form, one that makes questioning it an essential part of the experience.

The senior influential figure in this Biennial is Bruce Nauman, the conceptual artist who began working with language around 1966, not necessarily to reach a broader audience but rather to explore the material aspects of language. Whereas some conceptualists construed language in its raw essence as incorporeal, Nauman was among those who saw it as a sculptural medium. With his neon word pieces, which he began designing in the late 1960s, he literally turned ideas into objects by fabricating words out of colored glass tubing (fig. 4). One way in which Nauman brought conceptualism into the material world was to confer upon it an aesthetic vision that, so far as his neons were concerned, had more to do with cheap and tawdry advertising than it did with the traditions of art.

Nauman has worked with all kinds of media, including photography, film, video, sculpture, sound, and installation, but what unites his multifarious career is his abiding concern for what an artist is and, as he once said, "investigating the possibilities of what art may be."[9] For *Fantasy Underfoot*, Nauman contributed one work from his recent series of seven-projection video installations that document the nocturnal activity in and around his studio in Galisteo, New Mexico. Though strictly a document of the artist's workplace, the subject is ostensibly the proverbial space where all art is made, establishing this series as an exceptionally important one for

audiences, have multiple points of access, or draw upon diverse types of knowledge.[7] With installation, video, and film continuing to flourish, art today has so many points of entry that it is commonly described as spectacle and compared to entertainment. It is therefore as important as ever to understand not only *what* a work conveys but also *how*, that is, how a viewer relates to the object or experience. Indeed, if the present moment in art has a distinguishing characteristic, it is the new ways that the public figures into the design and presentation of the work. All of the art featured in *Fantasy Underfoot* invokes this issue of accessibility.

A case in point is *The Paradise Institute* (2001), by Janet Cardiff and George Bures Miller, one of the exhibition's featured installations, which offers the opportunity to enter a miniature theater and view a thirteen-minute suspense thriller. The film projected inside the theater employs certain obvious narrative strategies to capture viewers' attention, for example, the threat of danger or the anticipation of a sexual encounter. However, even with such stock rhetorical themes, this cinematic experience proves to be unlike any its audience has previously encountered. In addition to the Alice in Wonderland theatrical setting, there is a technologically advanced binaural soundtrack that may, according to one reviewer, revolutionize the way the artist, a manifesto of sorts that clarifies his place in the history of art since the 1960s.

Nauman made the video recordings during the summer of 2000, using infrared light, which gives the imagery, especially the eyes of the animals that populate the place, an eerie night-vision glow. For *Mapping the Studio II with color shift, flip, flop & flip/flop (Fat Chance John Cage) All Action Edit* (2001), the work featured in the present exhibition, he edited the raw footage so that only the so-called action would be projected. Mice scurry about, moths flitter, insects crawl, and the artist's cat, Toonsis, stalks, sometimes crying out in frustration, presumably for the rodents. Like the three other versions of "Mapping the Studio...," this installment reveals the secret drama where none would seem to exist, the poetic fantasy that is literally under Nauman's feet.

A number of artists in the exhibition—Linda Besemer, Marcel Dzama, Jacob El Hanani, Kojo Griffin, Nigel Poor, and Susan Smith-Pinelo—work in what are basically traditional, relatively intimate media, such as drawing, painting, photography, and, in the case of Smith-Pinelo, independent video, shown on standard 25- and 27-inch monitors.[10] The content of their work relates in various ways to the exhibition's thematic underpinnings, depending on its subject matter and metaphorical value. Linda Besemer's rigorous geometric paintings, for example, were made in the formal tradition of Piet Mondrian, Ellsworth Kelly, and Agnes Martin. As important contributions to that tradition, they are rich in art-historical allusions. However, displayed draped over aluminum rods, they may suggest bright and trendy designer dish towels in a mysterious and exalted form. The reference to domestic work is literal for El Hanani, who was inspired by one of his handy dish towels to make the stunningly compulsive drawing, *Dish Towel Grid* (2000). Besemer, like El Hanani, welcomes mundane associations such as these, which not only invite different levels of interpretation but also suggest the high and low character of modernist discourse.

The other artists—Cardiff and Bures Miller, Nancy Davidson, Ken Feingold, Tim Hawkinson, Nauman, and Bruce Yonemoto—may also work in cottage-industry fashion, or they may employ the help of professional fabricators and production assistants to create logistically complex works. In either case, the work of these artists is not intimate, but garish, spectacular, and interactive. Feingold's audio-animatronic mannequins actually communicate with one another or with museumgoers. In the case of Hawkinson's imposing, monsterlike creation, *Drip* (2002), the art is even aggressive and confrontational. Installation is the operative term here, as the experience of this work tends to be all-encompassing, making the idea of fantasy underfoot not only a matter of content but also, and perhaps more important, of form.

It is difficult to isolate the direct causes and effects that have given rise to the inviting conceptualism that characterizes the work in this exhibition. However, on some level there seems to be a degree of correlation between the accessibility or entertainment value of this art and the current state of museum practice, which, generally speaking, has been forced to compete with the larger field of popular diversions, ranging from movies to sporting events.[11] As a changing economy reduces traditional sources of funding, directors of all but a very few public museums are struggling to define programmatic visions that both satisfy their institutional mission and appeal to broader audiences. In these times, museums depend on their ability to attract visitors whose spending power has become increasingly crucial to their survival. The present essay is not the appropriate place to discuss which came first, entertainment-oriented contemporary art or the museums' need to exhibit such work. There is, in fact, a cultural context for the mutual support of such strategies by individuals and institutions. Contrary to the popular belief that all contemporary artists are determinedly esoteric, many of them do share the museums' preoccupation with expanding their audiences.

In an article about *Documenta 11*, the most recent in a series of important contemporary art expositions held in Kassel, Germany, every five years, critic Peter Schjeldahl described the event as yet another example of what he calls "festivalism": the "mixing of entertainment and soft-core politics" that does not demand contemplation but instead "invite[s], in passing, consumption of interesting spectacles."[12] Video, film, and computers— formats readily linked to television, movies, and other

fig. 4 Bruce Nauman, *SWEET SUITE SUBSTITUTE*, 1968 (fabricated 1982), red, yellow, and blue glass tubing, with clear glass tubing suspension frame, 5 ¹/₄ x 29 ³/₄ x 4 ³/₄". Gift of Mr. and Mrs. Bernhard G. Bechhoefer, Mr. and Mrs. William H. Draper, Mr. and Mrs. John D. Firestone, Mr. and Mrs. Lee M. Folger, Mr. and Mrs. Marvin Gerstin, Mr. and Mrs. John H. Hall, Jr., Hon. and Mrs. H. John Heinz, III, Mr. and Mrs. Joseph W. Henderson, Mr. and Mrs. Wallace F. Holladay, Mr. and Mrs. Freeborn G. Jewett, Mr. and Mrs. Gilbert H. Kinney, Mr. and Mrs. David Lloyd Kreeger, Mr. and Mrs. Michael Rea, Mr. and Mrs. Walter S. Salant, Dr. and Mrs. Stanley J. Sarnoff, Mr. and Mrs. B. Francis Saul, II, Mr. and Mrs. Brainard H. Warner, Hon. and Mrs. Sidney R. Yates, and with purchase funds from the William A. Clark Fund and the Mrs. Ethel B. Garrett Fund in honor of Jane Livingston

forms of mass entertainment—have played a large role in this general shift, contributing to artistic encounters of a new order: enormous-scale installations including digital projections and offering opportunities to play games and interact with computers or fiddle with video cameras, microphones, Palm Pilots, and the like. Though Schjeldahl is hard-pressed to identify art-historical precedents for this work, they can arguably be traced to the interactive installations and video projects of 1960s and 1970s conceptual artists such as Nauman, Robert Morris, Anthony McCall, and William Anastasi. In any case, we have now reached the point where one no longer simply examines an art object or what is displayed on a monitor. Instead, one is often required to find the end of the line, as with the Cardiff and Bures Miller installation, and wait for a turn to take in the experience or event.

The possibility that these kinds of artistic spectacles might be interesting, "just not too interesting," to quote Schjeldahl again, is perhaps their greatest risk. Indeed, how can a work of art that seems downright entertaining have serious value in intellectual, aesthetic, and historical terms? *Fantasy Underfoot* shows us that some of the best examples of this work are simultaneously immediate in their appeal and abstract, and that "getting it"—a cogent sense of the art's impact and importance—is an insight potentially available to the broadest possible audience. Here one thinks of the hundreds of thousands of people who make a point of visiting, or just happen upon, the many biennial, triennial, and other art festivals and exhibitions across the globe that are now a mainstay of the contemporary art world.

For his essay in this volume, U.S. Poet Laureate Billy Collins reminds us that "art offers us a place to stand as well as a doorway, if we choose to cross it, into the indeterminate." The potential for such transport may be fostered by a given work's surprise, beauty, shock, delight, horror, wonder, admiration value, or what have you. Whatever the cause, it is not necessarily limited to any medium, format or, for that matter, any particular segment of the population. This essay is, in part, an effort to show how art forms that are flourishing today owe much to the long-standing tradition of those made by artists who have sought to engage and move their audiences in important if not profound ways. The objects in *Fantasy Underfoot* not only have a place in that history of art but also suggest an investment in the historical role of the museum as a place where people come together to parlay the traditions of art into new forms, ideas, experiences, and, potentially, new social roles.

NOTES

1. I first read the phrase "conceptual vernacular" in the exhibition catalogue *Radical Scavenger(s): The Conceptual Vernacular in Recent American Art*, which features the artists Dan Graham, Mike Kelley, Louise Lawler, Cady Noland, Hirsch Perlman, Charles Ray, Ed Ruscha, and Christopher Williams. Richard Francis, the exhibition's curator, used the phrase to refer, on the one hand, to postmodern theory and, on the other, to a nonhierarchical approach to subject matter that does not, for example, give higher or lesser status to mundane and extraordinary subjects in relation to each other. In the present context the phrase is being used more generally. Conceptual is not meant to refer to a particular theory or theories but rather to the overt representation of ideas; vernacular is used to refer to standard, common, or familiar forms of communication. Richard Francis, *Radical Scavenger(s): The Conceptual Vernacular in Recent American Art* (Chicago: Museum of Contemporary Art, 1994), 11–12.

2. The word "movement" is used loosely here, as conceptual art practice during the 1960s and 1970s cannot be characterized definitively as a movement.

3. Blake Stimson, "The Promise of Conceptual Art," in *Conceptual Art: A Critical Anthology*, edited by Blake Stimson and Alexander Alberro (Cambridge, Mass.: MIT Press, 1999), xxxviii.

4. Lucy R. Lippard and John Chandler, "The Dematerialization of Art," *Art International* 12, no. 2 (February 1968): 31–36.

5. Writing about the work of Michael Asher, the art historian Thomas Crow called artistic strategies such as these "pastoral tricks": "By adopting what the great world would regard as limited points of view, it [certain kinds of discrete public interventions] achieves the largest possible comprehension and scale." Thomas Crow, "The Simple Life: Pastoralism and the Persistence of Genre in Recent Art," in *Modern Art in the Common Culture* (New Haven: Yale University Press, 1996), 194.

6. Among the many discussions of this aspect of conceptual art is that by Tony Godfrey, *Conceptual Art* (London: Phaidon, 1998), 15 and 163–70.

7. These points were made admirably by the "Conversations at The Castle" project of the 1996 Arts Festival of Atlanta. See Mary Jane Jacob, "Reaching the Goal: Curating Conversations," in *Conversations at the Castle: Changing Audiences and Contemporary Art*, edited by Mary Jane Jacob (Cambridge, Mass.: MIT Press, 1998), 17.

8. Ken Johnson, "Art in Review: Janet Cardiff and George Bures Miller," *New York Times*, 12 April 2002, E36.

9. Bruce Nauman, quoted in Coosje van Bruggen, *Bruce Nauman* (New York: Rizzoli, 1988), 7.

10. Smith-Pinelo's videos may be shown on monitors of varying sizes, but the artist prefers them to be between 19 and 29 inches.

11. See, for example, Philippe Vergne, ed., *Let's Entertain: Life's Guilty Pleasures* (Minneapolis: Walker Art Center, 2000), passim.

12. Organized by Okwui Enwezor, the fifth platform (or phase) of the 11th installment of the series was an exhibition that took place from 8 June to 15 September 2002. In addition to *Documenta 11*, festivalism may be used to describe any number of contemporary art exhibitions taking place both within and outside of museums today. See Adam Lerner's essay, "The Museum and the Multiplex," in this volume for a more extensive discussion of the topic, and Peter Schjeldahl, "The Global Salon: European Extravaganzas," *The New Yorker* 78, no.17 (1 July 2002): 94.

Study in Orange and White

I knew James Whistler was part of the Paris scene—
the café awning and the wicker chair—
but I was surprised when I discovered the painting
of his mother among all the colored dots
and jumpy brushstrokes
of the French Impressionists at the Musée d'Orsay.

And I was even more surprised
after a period of benevolent staring
to notice how the stark profile of that woman,
fixed forever in her chair,
began to resemble my own ancient mother
now fixed forever in the earth, the stars, the air.

I figured Whistler titled the painting
Arrangement in Gray and Black
instead of what everyone else calls it
to show he was part of the Paris scene,
but when I strolled along the riverbank,
after my museum tour,
I imagined how the woman's heart
could have broken
by being demoted from mother
to mere arrangement, a composition without color.

The summer couples leaned into each other
along the quay, and the wide boats
teeming with spectators slid up and down the Seine,
their watery reflections
lapping under the stone bridges,
and I thought to myself:
how fatuous, how off base of Whistler.

Like Botticelli calling *The Birth of Venus*
"Composition in Blue, Ocher, Green, and Pink,"
or the other way around,
like Rothko labeling one of his sandwiches of color
"Fishing Boats Leaving Falmouth Harbor at Dawn."

Or—as I scanned the menu at the café
where I had come to rest—
it would be like painting something droll,
say, a chef being roasted on a blazing spit
before an audience of ducks
and calling it "Study in Orange and White."

By that time, though, a waiter had appeared
with Pernod and a pitcher of water,
and so I sat thinking of nothing—
just watching the women and men
who were passing by,
mothers and sons walking their fragile dogs—
and of course, about myself,
a kind of composition in blue and khaki,
and, once I had poured
some water into the glass of anise—milky green.

Billy Collins

The Poetry Shuttle

Billy Collins, Poet Laureate of the United States, 2001–2003

Whenever a poem comes under discussion, whether it be in a classroom or a critical journal, it becomes "a patient etherised upon a table," to echo the words with which modern poetry is said to have begun. In a case such as this, when a poet brings his own poem under discussion, the results may be just as uncertain, the poem may be just as helpless and imperiled, but at least the doctor can claim some familiarity with the patient.

One advantage of this kind of self-analysis is that one can locate the biographical secret behind the poem. Many poems contain such a secret, which is often related to the poem's genesis, and which, curiously, is never a necessary part of the reader's experience.

"Study in Orange and White" began over lunch with my wife and friends at a restaurant in Domme, a small village in the Dordogne. On the cover of the menu that the waiter handed us was a curious illustration of a chef being roasted over a flaming spit (orange), while a small group of ducks (white) looked on. I took one of the menus home with me, thinking that this depiction of a comic reversal of the usual hierarchy of cooking might make a good book jacket. Back in Paris, a visit to the Musée d'Orsay triggered a poem about a Whistler painting, which somehow led me back to the ducks and the chef flambé.

I am usually more interested in how poems move than in what they might mean, and this poem moves around in a fairly characteristic pattern. Having little patience with poems whose opening lines thrust me into the middle of personal trauma or tie me in linguistic knots, I tend to begin with something familiar. The known is a portal into the unknown, and for the artist, the unknown is mainly what the finished piece will be. Here I start with one of the most recognizable paintings in Western art: Whistler's *Arrangement in Gray and Black*. The first movement away from the literal is the shift from Whistler's mother to mine, a slip into the autobiographical, an elegiac moment. The poem returns to Paris for a stanza and then moves off again into a speculation about Whistler's motives, his use of a very dry modernist title to lower the risk of sentimentality that painting your aged mom surely carries. A broader meditation on the relationship of titles to paintings follows. In the last stanza, the poem finds its way back to Paris and to me, the speaker, who is drawn into the world of paint as life copies or rather fuses with art.

This A-B-A pattern is the basic form of the Romantic lyric, which would typically begin in a landscape, move outward and/or inward, then return to the landscape, a scene now influenced by the intervening meditation. In my poem (really A-B-A-C-A), the local is a point of departure for imaginative and conceptual play as well as a destination that provides the reader with the same reassuring out-and-back movement of the popular song, or the blues for that matter. If the poem is a vehicle and the reader seeks transport, the preceding is a rough map of the journey.

Someone said that poetry should be clear to children and mysterious to adults—a striking observation that also provides two primary terms. I think of poetry as a kind of negotiation between the clear and the mysterious. Poems that offer me no delight usually fail to appreciate the distinction. What should be clear is made mysterious, confusing the reader, and what should remain mysterious is reduced to banality, deflating the reader's expectations and even deprecating his capacity for mystery. Sometimes obfuscation and simplification are disastrously combined in the same poem.

Both the literary and the plastic arts involve a shuttling back and forth from the concrete to the imaginative, from the ordinary to the newly created, and in this respect, they mirror the body-and-soul composition of our being. Perhaps the rides that art takes us on give us pleasure because aesthetic experience is so close to the way we experience the paradox of ourselves— bounded flesh and unlimited spirit. At the very least, art offers us a place to stand as well as a doorway, if we choose to cross it, into the indeterminate.

"Study in Orange and White" appears in Billy Collins's collection of poems Nine Horses, *published by Random House in 2002.*

The Museum and the Multiplex

Adam Lerner, Master Teacher, Modern and Contemporary Art, Denver Art Museum

Hey! You got chocolate in my peanut butter!

In criticizing the 2001 Venice Biennale, Benjamin Buchloh used the term "spectacle value" to describe contemporary art that deploys forms of engagement typical of mass culture.[1] Buchloh clearly has a negative view of this trend. "Media control in everyday life," he asserts, "is mimetically internalized and aggressively extended" into institutions of fine art. He objects to the authoritative aspects of media, but his attack reveals a more general concern: the infiltration of everyday life into the art museum, which is "defined as either exempt from or oppositional to mass-cultural regimes."[2] For Buchloh, film and video are not the only strategies of mass cultural communication that have infiltrated the museum. And if this issue is just part of a general concern about museums and the masses, it becomes more urgent to see if there is anything redeeming in the strategies he condemns. How does Buchloh's disparaging phrase "mass-cultural regimes" relate to what museum professionals call "visitor engagement" and "familiar sur-roundings"?[3] Is there something in the everyday world of mass culture beyond what Buchloh sees?

Art and Mass Culture

It doesn't require much experience with museums to sense that Buchloh is shouting into a wind that is blowing gustily in the opposite direction. Both art institutions and individual artists are increasingly capitalizing on strategies of communication found outside the supposedly protective walls of the museum. In the book *The Virtual and the Real: Media in the Museum*, filmmaker Selma Thomas recognizes that "television is a powerful and invasive tool." However, she argues that it is precisely for this reason that museums have the "responsibility" to "challenge this hegemony, to develop additional terms and examples, to provide new yet compelling visual information for our growing publics."[4] It is commonplace to point out that artists coming out of art schools today look more to television, popular film, design, fashion, and pornography than they do to the artists who preceded them. They are like the philosophers that G. W. F. Hegel associated with animals who "do not just stand idly in front of sensuous things" but "fall to without ceremony and eat them up."[5] This voracious appetite for mass culture, which reinforces a connection with the world at large, sometimes results in spectacular or multimedia works that seem to imitate the most successful commercial institutions in advanced economies. At other times, the steady diet of mass culture results in work that dares to show similarities to cartoons, pornography, or Hollywood films.

Janet Cardiff and George Bures Miller's willingness to traffic in familiar forms of mass entertainment speaks to the particular kind of defiance that can be found among contemporary artists. In their installation *The Paradise Institute* (2001), we climb into a fake theater, put on a pair of headphones, and watch a film, and are thereby transported to another reality. Actually, Cardiff and Bures Miller take us to two different places simultaneously. We seem to be watching an ordinary, though somewhat overdramatic, film, but at the same time we identify with whispering voices coming from the audience, voices that are talking about everyday matters. At some point, it is no longer possible to distinguish the staged characters in the film from those of reality, a feeling that is plainly enjoyable in an absorbing and unsettling way. Cardiff and Bures Miller know how to show us a good time, using all the tricks of Disneyland and Hollywood: the creation of a completely controlled environment, the use of sound as much as visual display to lead visitors into a fantasy place, characters we can identify with, and stories that are absorbing. Cardiff and Miller also make us think about what it means to identify with a work of fiction. Both the characters in the film and the characters in the audience are fictional, so we question what makes us empathize with one more than another. We enjoy the work in the same way we are accustomed to appreciating advanced works of high culture, as well as in the way we enjoy the familiar world of media in daily life.

One need read only a small portion of the criticism of any of the international biennials of the past few years to understand what works like Cardiff and Bures Miller's are defying. Aside from Buchloh, a certain segment of old-guard art intellectuals seems to see only the trivialization of art in these exhibitions and in the film and video works that have come to represent them.

"Amusement park" is probably the phrase most often used, but "Olympics," "variety show," "multiplex," and "music video" are other dismissive words found in the same issue of *Artforum* in which Buchloh launched his attack.[6] What these words and phrases share is an association with all forms of entertainment that are outside of the traditional fine-art context. Setting aside their obvious moralistic slant, these words betray a fear that art has become not simply unimportant but more like the cultural forms around it, more like the Olympics and the movies. The risk artists take is to make work that might be understood as entertainment. The weapon of their rebellion is pleasure.

The word "entertainment" now seems to be used in the same way that "decorative" was used thirty years ago to criticize painting. Clement Greenberg stated that "decoration is the specter that haunts modernist painting."[7] The danger was that once painting became abstract and lost any interest in depicting the world, it risked being indistinguishable from wallpaper or any other form of decoration designed to make one's surroundings more pleasing. In both instances, statements that presume to be about the quality of particular works of art serve to police the boundary around the category of art itself. The fact that there is no essential distinction between art and decoration or between art and entertainment makes it all the more important to insist on it. When art begins to look like decoration or entertainment, it loses what it depends upon most—its exclusivity.

The Disavowal of Pleasure

The desire to protect art's exclusivity would seem to explain the desire to dissociate art from pleasure. Cardiff and Bures Miller's work was singled out for praise in the 2001 Venice Biennale, because it was able, as one critic put it, to "integrate" into a more "complex way of thinking."[8] This statement recalls a distinction insisted upon by Hegel two centuries ago, which continues to influence thinking today. With one hand, Hegel eschewed works of art that "can be employed as a fleeting pastime to serve the ends of pleasure and entertainment"; with the other, he trumpeted art that could take its place alongside religion and philosophy as a means of revealing the "most comprehensive truths of the mind."

Hegel's distinction can be found in the writings of Theodor Adorno, who disparaged popular entertainment, or what he called the "culture industry," in favor of "knowledge or, better, a cognitive faculty of judging justly."[9] For both, aesthetic appreciation is defined by its very opposition to pleasure. This distinction suggests that implicit in the positive praise of Cardiff and Bures Miller's work for its complex thought is an appreciation that it does not simply give us pleasure. However, works like Cardiff and Bures Miller's could be viewed as engaging complex ways of *pleasing* just as much as complex ways of *thinking*. The *sociological* point that pleasure is commonly available, in such venues as sports arenas and amusement parks, and thought is associated with the limited world of scholarship seems to determine the *philosophical* argument for dissociating art from pleasure and connecting it to thought. In other words, the distinction between art and pleasure is a means of shoring up the boundary between the museum and the multiplex.

From a historical perspective, the art museum seems to embody this separation of art and pleasure.[10] No longer the pre-Enlightenment curiosity cabinet, with its array of artifacts, relics, and artworks, the modern museum categorized and distributed objects with more or less clean distinctions. Art historian Carol Duncan suggests that art museums were designed to manifest Hegel's desire for art to take its place alongside religion and philosophy. She argues that the birth of the modern art museum corresponded with aesthetic philosophies that attribute to art "the power to transform their viewers spiritually, morally and emotionally." According to Duncan, the primary characteristic of the modern museum is its separation from the realm of ordinary life. Looking at the development of the art museum since the eighteenth century, she states that it has primarily been committed to defining a "zone of time and space in which visitors, removed from the concerns of their daily, practical lives, open themselves to a different quality of experience."[11] Museums create "ritual" encounters with art to secure their isolation, or what she calls their "liminal" status. Identifying the victims and outlining the consequences of such a practice are the primary task of her provocative book, *Civilizing Rituals: Inside Public Art Museums*.[12]

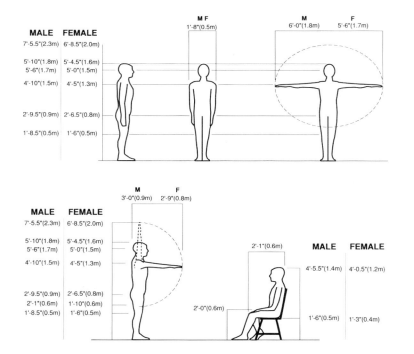

fig. 5 Basic human dimensions (adult). The illustrations accompanying this essay, all courtesy David Dean, are from his book *Museum Exhibition: Theory and Practice*. They remind us that while a frontline contingent of the museum focuses on a perilous encounter with mass culture, a rear-guard battalion is still fixed on a conflict where objects are threatened by the human body itself.

Placing Duncan and Buchloh side by side provides a fruitful comparison. For Duncan, the art museum's separation from everyday life permits it to present an art-historical narrative that addresses a very narrow type of visitor. She implies that people in everyday life maintain a diverse array of cultural attachments and that the art museum's isolation allows it to present itself essentially to a white male audience that it mistakenly claims is universal. Duncan's embedded suspicion of the museum's separation from everyday life contrasts with Buchloh's implicit belief in it. Their antithetical views occur because they have different conceptions of the everyday, of what the museum opposes when it builds its fortress walls. While Duncan believes there is a realm of social and political attachments outside of the commercial world, which needs to find a place within the museum, Buchloh sees the everyday as being overrun by commercialism and corporate interests.

Buchloh's case, that the museum has been invaded by commercial methods, seems to gain support by a mere glance at the Guggenheim Museum in New York. Great fanfare accompanied the appointment, in 1988,

of director Thomas Krens, who has a business degree from Yale. According to art journalist Deborah Solomon, Krens was known to refer to Marc Chagall and Paul Klee as "content."[13] Under his directorship, the Guggenheim Museum Bilbao, designed by Frank Gehry, has come to represent the most recent manifestation of the affinity between fine art and the tourist industry. The Las Vegas branch of the Guggenheim Museum allowed visitors to ride gondolas along an indoor canal before entering the spectacular curving space, also designed by Gehry, that housed its popular exhibition of Harley-Davidson motorcycles. The museum has been criticized for being too quick to water down its content in order to market it to American mass taste.

The more generous spin is that the Guggenheim is attempting to make its museums more inviting to new audiences. From this perspective, offering visitors a gondola ride before entering an exhibition is, in principle, not far from strategies pursued by museum education departments to engage ever-wider audiences. Museologist George Hein argues that by being "drawn into a theatrical process," museum visitors may acquire

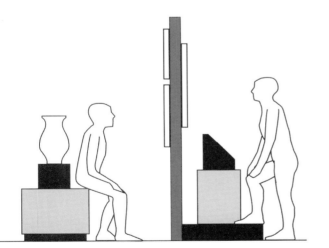

fig. 6 Sitting and leaning behavior.

greater "access to the content of the museum."[14] "Drama and theater," he states, "are gripping, powerful media to draw visitors into a scene"—a fact well known to Cardiff and Bures Miller. Strategies such as those suggested by Hein gain support from a body of evidence demonstrating that occasional visitors to museums value very different kinds of experiences from those valued by frequent museumgoers.[15] Museum marketing and public relations departments are charged with supporting the drive to reach more and more of these occasional visitors.

The Experience Economy

The fact that museums are moving closer to commercial institutions is matched by a long history of commercial enterprise approximating museum practice. In 1905 Herbert Croly, a founder of the *New Republic* and one of the founders of modern American liberal economics, wrote an article in the *Architectural Review* under the pseudonym A. C. David. In this article he championed a new cigar store in New York City, designed by the firm McKim, Mead and White, that called itself "The Finest Store in the World." Although unremarkable to us today, the notion that a store could be called "fine" was, in his words, "an absolute novelty."[16] Before then, "fine" was used to describe only the most esteemed works of culture, as in the term "fine art." For Croly, a fine store was an extraordinary innovation, because it demonstrated his hope that the future economy of America might be able to find a middle ground to replace both the patrician world of culture and the utilitarian world of commerce. This hope would soon be deflated, as a mass culture emerged from an economy largely governed by industries committed to mass production, with the realm of high culture primarily relegated to an increasingly marginal center, as it were.

A year after McKim, Mead and White completed the cigar store, they unveiled another building in New York, this one for a more typical client: the elegant Morgan Library, with its collection of rare books and masterpiece paintings. Today one sees a similar dichotomy in the civic and commercial architecture of Rem Koolhaas. This Rotterdam-based architect recently completed a store for Prada in New York City, costing approximately

$40 million, about as much as the new Contemporary Arts Center in Cincinnati, designed by the London-based architect Zaha Hadid. The most notorious element of the Prada store is its unpainted green plasterboard with white spackle, which turns out to be fake-unfinished, as the plasterboard Koolhaas preferred did not comply with the New York City fire code. It is not strictly elegance that Koolhaas was aiming for in the Prada store, but, according to critic Paul Goldberger, a mix of "common elements of popular culture with refined, high-end objects." It reminded Goldberger of the new Toys "R" Us store in Times Square, with its giant Ferris wheel in the center.[17]

According to Nike designer Gordon Thompson III, the development of the entertainment spectacle Nike Town in Seattle, in 1990, began the creative transformation of the retail industry that eventually resulted in the new Prada and Toys "R" Us.[18] Whereas department stores like Bergdorf Goodman, Macy's, and Bloomingdale's had previously promoted their images through their shops and brands, they degenerated into, as Thompson puts it, "Here's a hanger with something on it." Stores like Prada and Nike Town have substantially upgraded the utilitarian commercialism of shopping. However, these shops indicate that the middle ground of the American economy is centered not on refinement, as Croly wished, but rather on entertainment.[19]

In 1998, in a highly influential article in the *Harvard Business Review*, B. Joseph Pine II and James H. Gilmore argue that the leading edge of economic progress is characterized by corporations that are not selling goods but rather are "staging experiences" for consumers.[20] Not consciously referring to museums, they use key words that could just as likely have come from a "Visitor Studies" panel at an American Association of Museums conference. They describe their phenomenon as an instance when a corporation is able to "engage individual customers in a way that creates a memorable experience." Chuck E. Cheese and the Discovery Zone are examples of companies that have succeeded in creating memorable experiences for kids. Pine and Gilmore write approvingly that "at theme restaurants such as the Hard Rock Cafe, Planet Hollywood, or the House of Blues, the food is just a

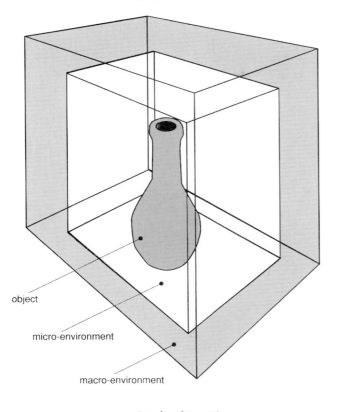

external environment

object

micro-environment

macro-environment

external environment

fig. 7 "Box-in-a-box" configuration of exhibition elements.

prop for what's known as 'eatertainment.'" The "experience economy" is clearly the future, they state, and "threatens to render irrelevant those who relegate themselves to the diminishing world of goods and services."

The art museum has a complicated place within the "experience economy." To begin with, museums are ahead of the game, since they have always been in the business of selling experiences, particularly the "ritual" or contemplative experiences that trouble Duncan. Of course, by Pine and Gilmore's standards, this is a relatively weak kind of experience, as it primarily involves "passive participation." They equate the experience of a museum visitor with that of a "tourist who merely views the Grand Canyon from its rim." Perhaps at one time a consensus of museum professionals would have approved of this description of the museum experience. It recalls Caspar David Friedrich's painting *Wanderer above the Mists* (c. 1818), which depicts a male figure standing at a grand precipice—an image that has come to represent the aesthetic experience. Pine and Gilmore

suggest that staged experiences also need to incorporate "active participation" and "absorptive" environments. And this is certainly a direction that museums are taking, not just with gondolas but with innovations like those recommended by George Hein.

For museums, the problem with the "experience economy" is that, according to Pine and Gilmore, "an experience occurs when a company intentionally uses services as a stage, and goods as props." This comes into direct conflict with art museum mission statements, which are far from defining collections as "goods" or "props." And call them what you will, you still can't touch them—at least most of them. Therefore, art museums are more limited than most cultural and commercial institutions in the kinds of experiences with objects that visitors are allowed to have. One solution adopted by more imaginative museum education departments is to create alternatives to their collection, spaces where visitors can touch and interact with objects in ways that would appeal to both museologist George Hein and businessmen Pine and Gilmore. In this instance, insofar as objects serve as "props" for active visitor experiences, they serve as surrogates, stand-ins for the things themselves. The predicament is that as art museums become engaging, more like the successful institutions around them, they turn farther away from their collections.

Provisional Answers Underfoot

At the outset of the twentieth century, Herbert Croly looked to the figure of the architect as the model for the new society, because the architect is "at once the artist, the professional and the businessman."[21] In fact, Croly claimed that his book *The Promise of American Life* was inspired by *The Unleavened Bread*, a novel whose hero is an architect struggling to maintain his ideals. For Croly, the architect embodied the ideal of everyday refinement that could unify the separate worlds of elite culture and common citizens. The problem is that Croly was never able to resolve how the architect could transmit his character to society at large. Therefore, *The Promise of American Life,* which is still referred to as one of the foundational texts for the modern American economy, amounted to a call for a society led by bureaucrats, with only the faintest hope that the architect-hero would set an example for others to follow.

Today architects and designers play a central role in the unifying forces of our economy, furthering the goals of both museums and commercial enterprises. In addition to Frank Gehry's dramatic structures, most new museum buildings around the world are designed to be spectacles in their own right. In this sense, they bear some similarity to the spectacular environments of Nike Town, Discovery Zone, and Prada. Croly wanted American society to be united as producers, but one hundred years later we seem more inclined to be consumers—of goods, of culture, of experiences. However, the spectacle need not be seen, as Buchloh would have it, as an invasion of commercial strategies into a protected realm. The spectacle emerges as a very specific architectural solution to the problems of the late-twentieth-century museum, as discussed above. The new art museum building separates itself from the everyday experiences of people on the basis of the type of

uncommon, memorable spectacle it creates. At the same time, it is able to engage wider audiences by offering them an immediately inspiring environment. Of course, the new museum architecture begs the question of what will fill it.

Fantasy Underfoot presents a number of artists who propose answers, at least provisionally, to the difficult questions regarding fine art and mass culture. Using strategies and forms borrowed from the broad spectrum of culture, they are creating art in which audiences find an inseparable mixture of pleasure, engagement, and thought. They demonstrate that an artist's individual aesthetic goals can coincide with the institutional goals of engaging new audiences. Selected from among the most advanced artists of our time, they dare to create work that bears similarities to TV and Hollywood film, comic books, interior design, and science fairs. They do so, in part, because they recognize the familiar pleasure in these forms, the same pleasure felt by the great mass of Americans. The artists in *Fantasy Underfoot* reach out to that crowd. In doing so, they help the museum connect with new audiences while contributing to an ongoing dialogue about the relationship between art and entertainment that is taking place throughout the contemporary art world.

NOTES

1. The ideas in this essay grew out of many conversations, both formal and informal, with my colleagues at the Denver Art Museum. I am grateful to all of them, especially to director Lewis Sharp, who encourages the staff to have these conversations; to Patty Williams, who suggested some of the bibliographical sources for this essay; and to Jeanne Hendrick, who supplied the epigraph.

2. Benjamin H. D. Buchloh, "Control, by Design," *Artforum* 40, no.1 (September 2001): 163.

3. See, for example, George E. Hein, *Learning in the Museum* (New York: Routledge, 1998), 160 and passim.

4. Selma Thomas and Ann Mintz, eds., *The Virtual and the Real: Media in the Museum* (Washington, D.C.: American Association of Museums, 1998), xi.

5. G. W. F. Hegel, *Phenomenology of Spirit*, trans. A. V. Miller (Oxford: Oxford University Press, 1977), 65.

6. *Artforum* 40, no.1 (September 2001): 155–87.

7. Quoted in Elissa Auther, "Clement Greenberg's Theory of the 'Decorative' and the Modernist Hierarchy of Art and Craft," unpublished manuscript, 2002. The argument in this paragraph directly follows the structure of the argument presented by Auther, who maintains that Greenberg distinguished between art and decoration under the pretense of separating good art from bad, but this distinction actually worked to secure the more essential boundary between art and nonart.

8. Similar phrases can be found throughout the critical literature, but this one appeared in Daniel Soutif, "Pick to Click," *Artforum* 40, no.1 (September 2001): 160.

9. This history of philosophical notions of pleasure and the accompanying quotes are drawn from Richard Shusterman, "Come Back to Pleasure," in *Let's Entertain: Life's Guilty Pleasures*, edited by Philippe Vergne (Minneapolis: Walker Art Center, 2000), 33–47.

10. Some of the most pleasurable art events in the nineteenth century were choreographed spectacles. The presentation of Albert Bierstadt's Western paintings and works such as Frederic Edwin Church's *Niagara* (1857) and Hiram Powers's *Greek Slave* (1846), both of which are in the collection of the Corcoran Gallery of Art, were popular events that took place in theaterlike settings where organizers charged admission. It should be noted that the museums that existed in the United States prior to 1870 were not like the institutions of today.

11. Carol Duncan, *Civilizing Rituals: Inside Public Art Museums* (New York: Routledge, 1994), 20.

12. Ibid., 130.

13. Deborah Solomon, "Is the Go-Go Guggenheim Going, Going…," *New York Times Magazine*, 30 June 2002, 36.

14. Hein, *Learning in the Museum,* 161.

15. Marilyn G. Hood, "Staying Away: Why People Choose Not to Visit Museums," *Museum News* 61, no. 4 (April 1983): 50–57; David Dean, *Museum Exhibition: Theory and Practice* (New York: Routledge, 1994), 19–31.

16. A. C. David [Herbert Croly], "The Finest Store in the World," *Architectural Record* 17 (January 1905): 42.

17. Paul Goldbeger, "High-Tech Emporiums," *The New Yorker*, 25 March 2002, 100.

18. Dike Blair with Elein Fleiss, "Fast on His Feet: Interview with Gordon Thompson III" (22 October 1996), in *Let's Entertain: Life's Guilty Pleasures*, 87.

19. There is substantial research on the historical relationship between the museum and the department store. See, for example, Carol Duncan, "Museums and Department Stores: Close Encounters," in *High-Pop: Making Culture into Popular Entertainment,* edited by Jim Collins (Malden, Mass. : Blackwell, 2002), 129–54.

20. B. Joseph Pine II and James H. Gilmore, "Welcome to the Experience Economy," *Harvard Business Review* 76, no. 4 (July–August 1998): 97–105.

21. Herbert Croly, "The Architect in Recent Fiction," *Architectural Record* 17, no. 2 (February 1905): 137.

Artists

Linda Besemer

- b. 1957, South Bend, Ind.
- lives and works in Los Angeles
- 4 paintings
- gallery 23

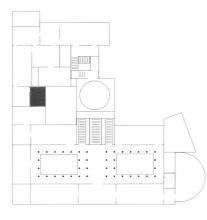

It was during the 1980s, while in art school, that Linda Besemer began searching for her own language as a painter. At that time, American art schools were still primarily teaching variants of formalism—theories that Besemer found limiting. This was particularly true for a young female artist interested in the feminist critiques of formalism then being developed. Besemer was especially attuned to critiques that construed the action of applying paint to canvas as a metaphor for an act of oppression, one that brought to mind, among other possible interpretations, male domination. Yet the representational and language-based conceptualism that was stepping in to replace formalism as the fashion du jour held little interest for Besemer. "I thought that a way to open up the limitations of both these discourses was to somehow eliminate or confuse the figure/ground binary," Besemer has said. "So I detached the paint from the canvas entirely. The supports for my paintings become a vehicle for the 'detachability' of the paint from different architectural grounds."[1]

Besemer found that acrylic can be readily detached from glass, and she began creating paintings whose surfaces were built up by applying layer after layer of acrylic paint. The first coats of paint laid down on the glass surface become one side of the finished painting—the first thing a viewer sees when encountering her work. The artist makes her tightly knit compositions more complex by building up the surface from front to back with lines that form, depending on the work, series of lines, grids, or spectrums of color. Once a pattern is complete, numerous layers of white paint are applied to create a ground for the first surface. After many layers, the white paint accumulates to the extent that it also becomes the ground for the second surface. The center layers of white paint, the painting's core, mark the distinction between the two surfaces (front and back and top and bottom), but also uniquely bind them in a shared ground. The second surface, or back, is painted directly onto the built-up layers of the first surface. When the second surface is finished, the painting is removed from the glass as one object—with two sides and one shared ground. The paintings, acrylic through and through, have two front sides and they remain elastic.

Besemer displays her padlike paintings in a variety of ways. In this exhibition they are draped over aluminum rods affixed to the wall. At first glance, viewers often assume that these double-sided soft works are some sculptural medium other than paint. Indeed, because we are conditioned to think that paintings require a support—canvas, board, paper, or wall—experiencing Besemer's work may subvert our expectations. Her rigorous and technical approach to the discipline produces astonishing results.

Besemer's slick and mysterious objects inspire a desire to touch that clearly separates them from the sterility associated with traditional formalist painting. The scrupulous, brightly colored geometric patterns suggest doctrinaire formalist theory, but draped casually on aluminum rods, they evoke the sphere of the everyday. The cerebral and pristine nature of the grid gives way to forms that feel tangible, unauthoritative, and even seductive. Bright summer colors and patterns like those in *Fold #55* (2001; fig. 8) bring to mind hand towels draped over the handle of an oven or beach accessories—vinyl tote bags, rubber flip-flops, and the classic striped beach blanket. Other color schemes, as in *Fold Quadrant #5* (2001; fig. 9), which contains the basic primaries red, blue, and yellow, and also integrates light blue, lavender, and black grids, seem to convey a more serious tone, suggesting traffic patterns or computer data.

The composition of the paintings appears to be virtually perfect, but upon closer inspection, it becomes obvious that the patterns on the two front sides are intentionally misaligned, often to dizzying effect. For example, a single line may weave over and under others to create an illusion of depth. But the details are such that the net effect is an almost machinelike precision. Besemer has been heavily influenced by the work of Eva Hesse, who experimented a great deal with malleable resins. Besemer, like Hesse, is interested in the flexibility of materials and their display. Her paintings are at

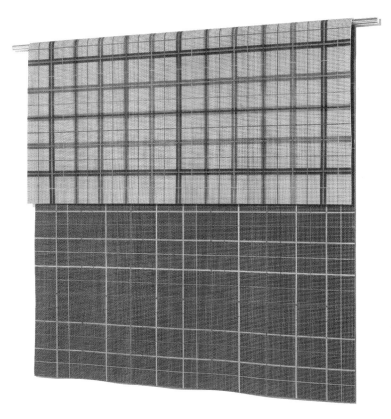

fig. 8 *Fold #55*, 2001, acrylic paint over aluminum rod, 72 x 80^1/$_8$ x 2". Courtesy the artist and Angles Gallery, Santa Monica, Calif.

once geometric in shape and pattern and organic in their structure, which can be slightly rippled at times.

Besemer successfully merges evocations of women's domestic work with the intellectual underpinnings of traditional painting. Her glossy, overscaled "folds," "zips," and "slabs," as she refers to the different shapes her paintings may take, move easily between complementary and dissonant color schemes; their folds and curves imply a potential for movement. Because of their economical use of material and form, Besemer's paintings are exceedingly elegant, offering immediate visual pleasure. Yet they also mine a deep vein in the history and tradition of painting, a juxtaposition that, in Besemer's hands, is uniquely satisfying.

Stacey Schmidt

1. Linda Besemer, quoted in "Too Colorful: A Conversation with David Batchelor," in *Linda Besemer* (New York: Cohan Leslie and Browne, 2002), 21.

Linda Besemer

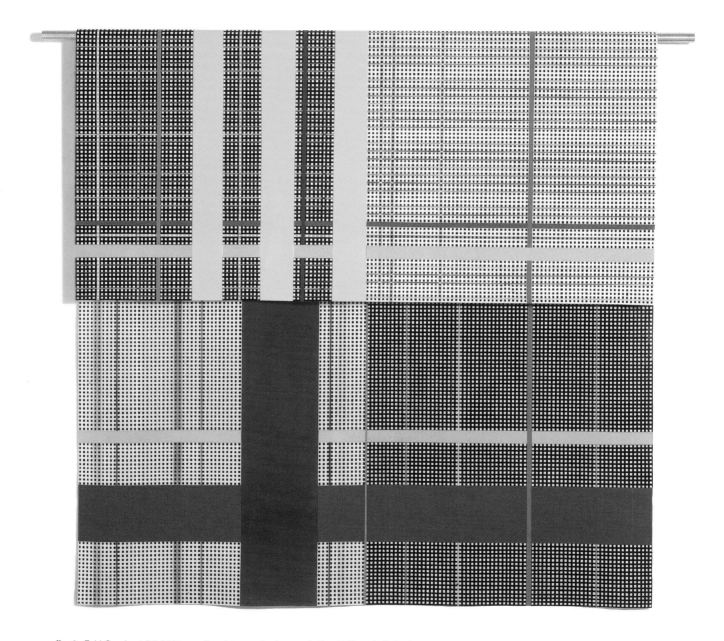

fig. 9 *Fold Quadrant #5*, 2001, acrylic paint over aluminum rod, 73 x 80 $\frac{1}{8}$ x 2". Collection of Phyllis and John Kleinberg

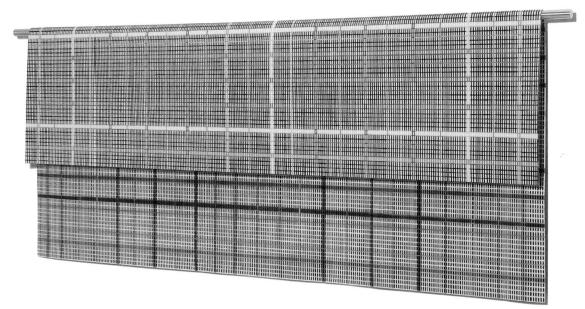

fig. 10 *Fold #54*, 2001, acrylic paint over aluminum rod, 32 x 76 ^{1}/$_8$ x 2". Collection of Mr. and Mrs. Frank Herringer

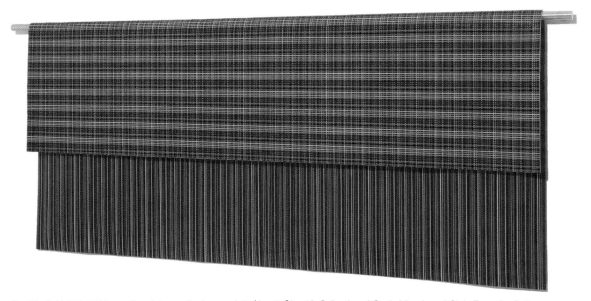

fig. 11 *Fold #56*, 2001, acrylic paint over aluminum rod, 31 ^{1}/$_2$ x 76 ^{3}/$_8$ x 2". Collection of Curtis Liberda and Chris Esworthy, Dallas

Janet Cardiff and George Bures Miller

Janet Cardiff
- b. 1957, Wingham, Ontario, Canada
- lives and works in Lethbridge, Alberta, Canada, and Berlin

George Bures Miller
- b. 1960, Vegreville, Alberta, Canada
- lives and works in Lethbridge, Alberta, Canada, and Berlin

- 1 multimedia installation
- gallery 25

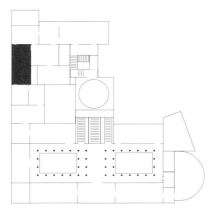

The Paradise Institute (2001) mischievously explores the relationship between reality and fiction. We enter a plain-looking plywood box and sit down in what looks exactly like the balcony of a grand movie theater. The seats are of red velvet, and the floor is raked like that of an actual theater balcony. Looking toward the front, we see the rest of the theater foreshortened, giving the illusion of viewing a huge screen from very far away, when, in fact, we are looking at a tiny screen from very close up. The film begins, and while a dark mystery appears to be unfolding on the screen, a whispering voice, seemingly coming from right beside us, asks if we want some popcorn. Later that same voice asks if we have checked the stove before leaving the house. Along with the story unfolding on the screen, another story is apparently being told, through audio, that involves the audience. However, as the two stories progress, we realize that it is difficult to distinguish between them. Strangely, we hear what sounds like the audience counting, in unison, "267, 268. . . . ," and we see a burning house on the screen, which may be our own house, whose stove we left on. Finally, we hear banging on the outside of our plywood box and are told to leave the theater, but the voice giving the command is that of the sinister character we were just watching on the screen.

Cardiff and Bures Miller's film installation differs from a typical Hollywood film in the same way that a murder-mystery weekend differs from a typical Broadway play. When you watch a traditional play, you may become absorbed in the story, but the illusion is always confined to the stage. When you participate in a murder-mystery weekend, you have dinner at a hotel, where someone is ostensibly murdered, and you have to figure out who did it, so you are the person onstage. It is the difference between watching *Star Wars* in a cinema and visiting Space Mountain at Disneyland. It is like having a blackout while at home alone watching a scary movie late at night; you become immersed in the fiction.

The difference between Cardiff and Bures Miller's work and popular escapist forms of entertainment is that the latter build an imaginary world that is consistent. In *The Paradise Institute*, you do not simply become one character in a coherent fantasy; instead, you can never tell what story you are being woven into and where the illusionism ends. As soon as you begin to make sense of what is being experienced—okay, now I'm watching a thriller and that guy is really in trouble; okay, now I'm listening to another member of the audience—the rug is pulled out from under you, and you realize that the member of the audience is also part of the thriller. You don't know what is supposed to be reality and what a dream, who is supposed to be an actor and who a member of the audience.

The Paradise Institute belongs to a tradition of Brechtian theater in contemporary art that aims to break down the barrier between audience and actors. When John Cage composed *4'33"*—which calls for a performer to sit at a piano for four minutes and thirty-three seconds without playing a note— he asked audiences to listen to the sounds all around them, the sounds of people rustling in their seats, breathing, coughing. Cage forced audiences to recognize that this is not simply noise,

fig. 12 Exterior view of *The Paradise Institute*, 2001, multimedia installation, 120 x 449 x 201". Courtesy Luhring Augustine, New York, and Galerie Barbara Weiss, Berlin; view of installation at Hamburger Bahnhof, Berlin

which interferes with the true sound of the performance, but is itself legitimate and interesting sound in its own right. When Vito Acconci, in a performance, stared at every member of the audience in turn for thirty seconds, he was similarly reminding his viewers that they, too, were part of the performance. Cardiff and Bures Miller take audiences to new levels of immersion. They remind us that we cannot rely on the distinction between illusion onstage and reality offstage, since the performance entirely surrounds us. They make us see how easily we fall back into illusionism, believing that there really is a fourth wall to the stage that separates us from them.

The Paradise Institute is similar to earlier works by Cardiff and Bures Miller. Cardiff created numerous "walks," where visitors don headphones and sometimes carry video cameras as they are guided through various spaces from museum galleries to city streets. These works explore intersubjectivity: our ability to experience the world from another's point of view. As Cardiff states in *Louisiana Walk* (1996), "We're connected now, my breath a part of yours, my thoughts transferred to your mind." These works also explore how we give meaning

to the world. Through the voice of another, ordinary objects and places trigger memories and associations. We are made to see that what we think is the real world is actually overcoded with our own fantasies.

Bures Miller's past work also plays with the traditional conventions of narrative cinema. In *Conversation/ Interrogation* (1991), the viewer sits in a chair and watches a person in the film talk to someone offscreen. When the camera crosscuts to the person offscreen, the viewer sees him/herself, captured on a surveillance camera. As in his collaborative work with Cardiff, Bures Miller involves us literally in his projects, toying with our expectations that the imaginary world of cinema is experienced through an imaginary window, separating us from the world of fiction. In *The Paradise Institute*, Cardiff and Bures Miller create an environment that manifests the interests of both artists, where visitors create identifications only to have them destabilized, where their expectations about the boundary between reality and illusion are undermined at every turn.

Adam Lerner

Janet Cardiff and George Bures Miller

Janet Cardiff and
George Bures Miller

fig. 13 Interior view of *The Paradise Institute*, 2001. Courtesy Luhring Augustine, New York

Nancy Davidson

- b. 1943, Chicago
- lives and works in New York
- 1 inflatable site-specific installation
- north atrium

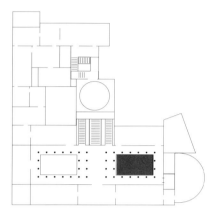

For nearly ten years, Nancy Davidson has been creating seductive and slyly ironic, gargantuan inflatable sculptures from latex weather balloons "dressed" in risqué outfits. Their oversized forms bring to mind buoyant breasts and salacious bottoms, and the titles have frequently invoked hypersexualized icons like Mae West and Betty Boop. But Davidson has also suggested they can evoke hybrids of newborns, old men, children, and animals. Regardless of specific association, all of Davidson's works draw from the rich subjects of humor and the grotesque.

Coming of age in the late sixties and early seventies, Davidson became interested in, and influenced by, minimalism. However, her desire to create work that could generate a variety of associations and emotions while speaking to a wide audience compelled her to take an "additive" approach to the pared-down visual vocabulary of traditional minimalist forms. By increasing the scale and aesthetic impact of her objects, Davidson sought to pique the interest of an audience unfamiliar with contemporary art while remaining steeped in an art-historical dialogue with minimalism.

Davidson's solution came from two sources. Her love of soft materials and forms helped plant the seed that grew into her eventual use of balloons. And the writings of Mikhail Bakhtin on Rabelais and carnival suggested that instead of merely breaking down the barriers posed by minimalism, she could subvert the barriers through forms of grotesque humor that were at once powerful and anti-authoritative.

Davidson's use of humor allies her with a number of other contemporary artists working in this vein. Finding a language that would be unique and separate from the patriarchal voice in art was an important part of the feminist art movement during the late 1960s and 1970s, and Davidson picked up this historic thread in her work. Like contemporaries such as Ida Applebroog, Marie Baronnet, and Nancy Spero, Davidson sought to break down stereotypes by using humor to dislocate representations of the body—both male and female. She points out, however, that she does not pursue a particular agenda through her art, and she is not interested in characterizing her audiences as having specific reactions to the work. In her words, "It is open and giving, ready for all." [1]

Inspired by the art of Eva Hesse and interested in its possibilities, Davidson sent away for a weather balloon. "The minute it came I blew it up and knew immediately it was the perfect material. Funny, grotesque, huge, erotic, absurd, attractive, and a body with flesh and very importantly a body of parts, male, female. . . . We all have these bulbous parts."[2] The balloons—trussed with ropes, bulging from lace, constrained by thongs, hanging, floating, rolling, popping out of corsets, lidded as "carnival eyes"—have become a perfect evocation of both the human body and the human condition. The flimsy materials, the struggle with gravity, the delicate stasis between inflation and contraction, and the inflation nozzles, which are sexually ambiguous in their phallic appearance and receptive function, contribute to sculptures that read as female yet retain a sense of being crossgendered. The grotesque excess of bulging "flesh" in Davidson's work also functions to critique common stereotypes: "big is beautiful" riffs off minimalism's "less is more."

fig. 15 *Study #2 for Double Exposure* (detail), 2002, photomontage, 7 9/16 x 7".
Courtesy the artist and Robert Miller Gallery, New York

Created especially for the Corcoran's 47th Biennial, *Double Exposure* (2002) is Davidson's largest inflatable project to date. During a preliminary site visit to the museum in 2001, the artist was particularly intrigued by the columns and colonnades of the Beaux-Arts atrium, as well as the neoclassical marble busts that line the walls. Her installation effectively bisects the skylit court of the north side of the Museum, creating two unique spaces, one below and one above the hanging form. *Double Exposure* is less overtly sexualized than many of Davidson's other works: a clean minimalist form seemingly suspended, and constricted, by a massive blue rope anchored into the skylight above.

The space created below is defined by the looming, enormous soft form, which glows from within and hangs only a few feet above the viewer's head, just out of reach. The atrium walls were painted pink for the installation, and the permanently displayed nineteenth-century American marble busts were rearranged so that only females are present near the hanging form. The overall effect is both strangely nurturing and oppressive. The hovering work seems evocatively womblike, an impression strengthened by the pink walls, the constricted feeling of the space, and the exposed milky-white breasts of the nearby marble busts. Warm and intimate, the balloon seems to nurture

and protect the viewer through its proximity. Yet the form's bound rope removes the work from the realm of the motherly, leaving an ambiguous, if not threatening, impression. From below, it is impossible to tell whether the balloon is suspended or is actually floating.

Seen from above, the work takes on an entirely different appearance. The smooth curves of the balloon rise over the railings of the mezzanine like some kind of cherry-red landscape, looming like small hills within the Museum's traditional Beaux-Arts interior. The now-obvious fact that the piece is suspended from the ceiling changes the viewer's perception of it, perhaps replacing an interpretation of nurturing motherhood with one involving some form of bound erotica. Many possible interpretations are left open for viewers, and that is fine with Davidson. "I believe we are all attracted to the signifiers of our shared bodies. Excess attracts and repulses, invoking and thwarting fetishized desire."[3]

Stacey Schmidt

1. Nancy Davidson, artist's statement, 2002.

2. Ibid.

3. Ibid.

Nancy Davidson

fig. 16 *Study #3 for Double Exposure*, 2002, photomontage, 7 $^9/_{16}$ x 11 $^{15}/_{16}$". Courtesy the artist and Robert Miller Gallery, New York

Marcel Dzama

• b. 1974, Winnipeg, Manitoba, Canada
• lives and works in Winnipeg
• 174 drawings
• gallery 25

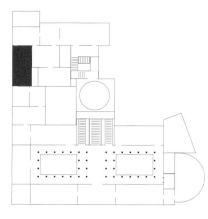

Marcel Dzama's art politely invokes the recent past while letting the viewer peer into some kind of alternate future reality. The cast of human and partly human characters that populate his drawings is vast, and there are families of figures that frequently reappear. At the very least, we can from time to time count on seeing a relative of Dzama's "puffy man" or the "tree guy." This familiarity leads us to believe there must be a clear narrative embedded within the hundreds of untitled works that he pins to the wall simultaneously—a thread to follow from page to page. Dzama tells us, however, that "there is a narrative, but it's so muddled that it's like an inside joke that has gone too far."[1] It is up to the viewer, then, to construct any number of possible scenarios from the somewhat random order imposed by a given installation. Dzama provides the raw visual material but leaves the interpretations to one's imagination.

The illustrational quality of Dzama's work is undeniable. His art is a unique hybrid of comic strips and old picture books from our collective youth. The thinly outlined figures exhibit petite, quirky features that call to mind the drawings of Edward Gorey; and, indeed, Dzama and Gorey share a love of the bizarre and a fondness for the morose. Through the direction of their line work, they have a remarkable ability to convey deadpan humor that is often utterly dark.

With their smartly cut bobs and smock dresses, many of Dzama's girls resemble flappers, while others, in face masks and rubber suits, straddle the thin line between superheroes and S&M enthusiasts. His tableaux, and many of the girls themselves, also are reminiscent of outsider artist Henry Darger's crime-fighting, polysexual Vivian Girls, themselves traced from old advertisements for children's clothing ads and Sears Roebuck catalogs. Like the Vivian Girls, Dzama's ladies travel in packs, wearing identical clothing and the same helmetlike hairstyle; they have a penchant for cute outfits and guns, along with a distaste for boys that borders on the murderous. Their similar features indicate they are a clique, clearly working as part of the same task force. A group may have a ringleader, as in one drawing (2002; fig. 17) that depicts a girl set slightly apart from the others, wearing a long-sleeved rather than a sleeveless dress and standing with an assertive posture. She

fig. 17 *Untitled*, 2002, watercolor on paper, 14 x 11". Courtesy the artist and David Zwirner, New York

this brew an incredible tonal range, from cinnamon to mahogany. Red makes a limited appearance wherever blood and guts are called for; it is not unusual to see severed limbs and bleeding wounds—the work of knife-wielding monkeys and gun-toting Martians. Yet a tension is created by combining this explicitly cartoonish violence with Dzama's nuanced illustrations and delicate gouache brushwork.

Sexual scenarios run rampant. Take, for instance, the picture of the tightly knit group of female figures standing around the quite confident, hand-on-his-hip tree guy (fig. 21). Their coy smiles and girlish stances indicate a giggling admiration for this tall, barked rogue. His sophisticated, chest-hugging plaid shirt with the flipped-up collar, pencil pants, and Beatle boots mark him as the sort of guy inevitably named "Chip" in many books of our youth. But what are we to make of this (otherwise) refined, pipe-smoking fellow's happy response to the fact that the demented-looking man beside him is sans trousers?

The fact that Dzama's works are typically pinned to the wall rather than framed seems to indicate an unpretentious familiarity that makes the visuals all the more effective at knocking the viewer off balance. These pages can be thought of as playgrounds for the absurd—Rorschach images in which we confront, head on, our fears and unspoken desires. Dzama's drawings invite us in with their clean illustrative style and seemingly familiar details, so that we find ourselves taken for a ride and swept up into Dzama's eccentric imagination.

Stacey Schmidt

appears to be the one responsible for ensuring the safety of a now-headless monkey (her sidekick?), which looks as if it has just been victimized. As her posse of girls preoccupy themselves with other things—brushing their hair and hemline needlework—she forges ahead, knife in hand, determined to teach a lesson to her adversary, an overgrown boy scout. In the end, it is difficult to discern who are the good and who are the evil-doers, if indeed there are any, in this scenario.

Dzama's color schemes seem as if they were drawn almost directly from the vintage era of *Highlights for Children* magazine, when two- and three-color printing, using the greens, browns, and grays then popular, was the norm. The artist uses an extract of root beer in mixing his browns, and he has managed to tease out of

1. Adam McEwen, "People are strange: Adam McEwen on Marcel Dzama," *Frieze* (May 2001): 66–67.

Marcel Dzama

Marcel Dzama

fig. 18 *Untitled*, 2002, watercolor on paper, 14 x 11". Courtesy the artist and David Zwirner, New York

fig. 19 *Untitled*, 2001, watercolor on paper, 14 x 11". Courtesy the artist and David Zwirner, New York

fig. 20 *Untitled*, 2002, watercolor on paper, 14 x 11". Courtesy the artist and David Zwirner, New York

fig. 21 *Untitled*, 2002, watercolor on paper, 14 x 11". Courtesy the artist and David Zwirner, New York

Jacob El Hanani

- b. 1947, Casablanca, Morocco
- lives and works in New York
- 12 drawings
- gallery 14

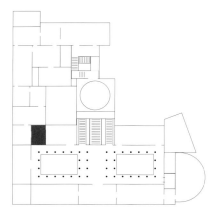

Seeing Jacob El Hanani's works lining the wall for the first time, one may view them as gray monochromatic fields of varying densities. Whether a trick of the brain or the eye, or a combination of the two, we are conditioned as viewers to resolve in an instant the mystery of how an image is made. In El Hanani's case, precedent also convinces us to read these particular images as part of the lineage of minimalism, to which they seem closely allied. Painter and critic Ad Reinhardt, an important influence on the minimalists, wrote in 1963: "The one object of fifty years of abstract art is to present art-as-art and as nothing else, to make it into the one thing it is only, separating and defining it more and more, making it purer and emptier."[1] At first glance, Reinhardt's often-cited statement seems appropriate in the context of El Hanani's work.

One has to look very closely, and strain one's eyes a bit, to discover that El Hanani's mind-blowing drawings are anything but empty. Each work is composed of thousands of tiny lines arranged in connecting patterns—motifs ranging from dots, circles, crosshatching, and shifting grids to minute Hebrew calligraphy—crossing the surface in almost microscopic detail. In many of the drawings the lines are so tiny and so nearly perfect that it is difficult to believe El Hanani's marks are handmade.

Looking deeper, however, one can perceive the imperfections that are the mark of human endeavor. The pen rests in one place a moment too long, and the result is a darkened line in the midst of lighter marks. A change in the angle of the hand results in a barely noticeable thickening of a line that becomes a tiny edge in the overall composition. El Hanani embraces these imperfections and the unpredictability they impose on his compositions. In this, he has little in common with the artists who gave definition to minimalism in the mid-1960s—Carl Andre, Donald Judd, Dan Flavin, Sol LeWitt, Robert Morris, and Anne Truitt. Although El Hanani admits that minimalism was a prime influence when he arrived in New York in the mid-1970s, he argues that his work is just the opposite—"maximalist." Reacting to the minimalists' dictum that the idea is more important than the execution, El Hanani began spending up to six months completing a single drawing. The irony is that the resulting works are read as minimalist due to their accumulation rather than their reduction of details.

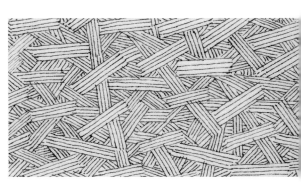

fig. 22 *Basket (from the "Basket" series)*, 2002, ink on paper, 32 1/8 x 40 1/16". Courtesy Nicole Klagsbrun Gallery, New York

fig. 23 *Basket* (detail), 2002. Courtesy Nicole Klagsbrun Gallery, New York

Using either a quill or a superfine Rapidograph pen and India ink, El Hanani fills a paper no more than two square feet in size with a density of markings that would be almost impossible to surpass. On more than one occasion, El Hanani has said, "Jackson Pollock used his shoulder, and other artists used the wrist, so I decided I would use only the tip of my finger." The artist never uses a magnifying glass and says he can work for no more than twelve to fifteen minutes at a time before needing a break to rest his eyes and hand. The marks he makes are so small that the weather variations in humidity, temperature, and air pressure require him to use different papers, inks, and writing instruments to achieve the desired effect.

Jacob El Hanani was born in colonialist Casablanca, growing up in a rich mix of cultures and religious traditions—Jewish, Muslim, and Christian—that has continued to inform his work. He has remarked that his practice of repetition as a youth, such as repeating a prayer four or five times a day, has filtered into his art. It is difficult to determine which had more influence on his small textural works, the mezuzah—a parchment scroll inscribed with writings from the Jewish Scripture that is placed in a small case—or the tradition of Islamic miniature painting. The slow pace of Islamic life in Casablanca had an enormous effect on his working method. "Time was abandoned," he says, as his mother and grandmother spent entire afternoons cooking savory food filled with spices. The intricacy and ornamentation of the Jewish and Islamic household items he grew up with—textiles,

baskets, tile paintings, carved screens—help to explain why El Hanani works the way he does.

Alef-Beth-99-2000 (1999–2000; fig. 26) is characterized by a loose arrangement of rectangular forms, which are composed of Hebrew letters (Alef-Beth is Hebrew for "alphabet"). For El Hanani, the soft curves of the Hebrew language "liberate" him from the straight rigors of the Latin alphabet. There is no Hebrew message to decode, however, as he focuses mainly on the abstract use of the alphabet, whose images are as mutable as the shifting sand outside Casablanca. For this particular work, he began with a letter and repeated it a set number of times across different lines until a small box was formed. He then rotated the sheet of paper and continued with another letter until a second box formed, continuing in this manner until the sheet was filled.

Philosopher and critic Arthur Danto has described El Hanani's images as "so tiny that they put one in mind of a person dedicated to inscribing the Koran on a grain of rice. The drawings evoke peace and patience, as if time had no bearing on their world."[2] These are fitting words for an artist who has been working consistently at his own pace for almost three decades.

Stacey Schmidt

1. Ad Reinhardt, "Art-as-Art," *Art International* (20 December 1962), quoted in C. Dorothy Miller, ed., *Americans 1963* (New York: Museum of Modern Art, 1963), 82.

2. Arthur C. Danto, "Best of 2000," *Artforum* (December 2000): 112.

Jacob El Hanani

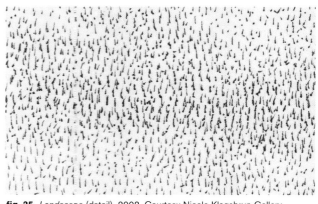

fig. 25 *Landscape* (detail), 2002. Courtesy Nicole Klagsbrun Gallery, New York

fig. 24 *Landscape*, 2002, ink on paper, 32 1/8 x 40 1/16". Courtesy Nicole Klagsbrun Gallery, New York

fig. 27 *Alef-Beth-99-2000* (detail), 1999–2000. Courtesy Nicole Klagsbrun Gallery, New York

fig. 26 *Alef-Beth-99-2000*, 1999–2000, ink on paper, 22 1/2 x 28 1/2". Courtesy Nicole Klagsbrun Gallery, New York

Ken Feingold

- b. 1952, Pittsburgh
- lives and works in New York
- 3 computer-driven sculptural installations
- gallery 22

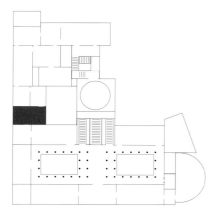

Throughout his career, Ken Feingold has explored a series of key philosophical and existential questions in relation to different forms of representation. Trained at Antioch College and California Institute of the Arts between 1970 and 1976, Feingold worked primarily with film, video, and sculpture in the 1970s and 1980s, sometimes recycling these media and combining them in larger and more encompassing installations. His focus on installations has recently increased, and the computer has become an integral part of his art since 1990. By learning to program and configure computer networks, Feingold became one of the pioneers of interactive art, a form of contemporary cultural practice that creates temporally unfolding works that use complex forms of technology to incorporate the responses of diverse viewers into their aesthetic structures.

One of interactive art's most innovative practitioners, Feingold displays an ironic if somewhat dark sense of humor in his installations. His dadaist or surrealist sensibility seeks to provoke experiences of the uncanny—moments when fear and wonder are combined and the world appears both familiar and strange—as a means to explore both contemporary society and technology's effect on the psyche. Feingold's surrealism is most evident in his obsessive use of puppets and dummies, conflicted stand-ins for himself and others, which he animates through mechanical, electronic, and pneumatic systems. His debt to dada—the international "anti-art" movement that spawned surrealism—may be seen in his love of kitsch and pop culture (particularly science fiction), his focus on audience interactivity, and his exploration of randomly generated and collaborative means of experimental poetry. At the same time, Feingold's sensibility remains his own, mediated by his long-standing interests in structural cinema, experimental video, conceptual art, philosophy, and theory.

Sinking Feeling (2001; fig. 28) consists of a talking animatronic head in a flowerpot on top of a small nightstand, a head that allows viewers to "communicate" with it by means of a microphone placed a few feet away. Through simple forms and comic juxtapositions that connote the practices of genetic engineering, the work broaches the question of how humans can interact and communicate with computers and machines. Here, as in

fig. 28 *Sinking Feeling* (detail), 2001, multimedia installation, 52 x 15 x 18", installation dimensions with projection variable. Courtesy Postmasters Gallery, New York

Self Portrait as the Center of the Universe (2001; fig. 29) consists of a series of sculptural and audiovisual elements that create a cinematic space wherein we listen to a conversation between an animatronic portrait head of the artist and a virtual head projected onto a screen facing the animatronic effigy. Driven by two slightly different personality algorithms, the two heads converse; their conversation drives a sequence of cyclical digital "loops"—bits of "collapsed time," as the artist calls them—images that have biographical or symbolic significance. Within the projection, which includes both the digital head (or "alter ego") and the loops, software-driven three-dimensional animations also circulate. The projected digital imagery is natural but is often concerned with death. As the conversation develops, the trees and waterfalls are juxtaposed with bodies and massive piles of skulls. The work evokes a sense of the world as being divided into egos and copies, followers and leaders. The projected alter ego is often surrounded by smaller heads that move in lockstep around it, and the sculptural Feingold head is presented on a saucer-like table amid a group of distressed ventriloquist dummies that the artist purchased on eBay. Both "sides" of Feingold's self-portrait—the three-dimensional animatronic effigy and the two-dimensional projected alter ego—seem to create paradoxical manifestations of "themselves," a process of self-replication that suggests both communication and the formation of armies.

If/Then (2001; fig. 30), like *Self-Portrait. . . ,* explores the interactivity of machines, this time with seemingly less connection to Feingold's own psyche or ego. Here two animatronic female heads, each positioned with her mouth to the other's ear, converse in a cardboard box filled with Styrofoam packing material. The sculptural elements suggest a factory of the future where intelligent robots are produced. One box appears to have been taken off the assembly line, the identical heads dislodged and turned on. Through a rambling conversation driven by their rudimentary artificial intelligence, they now attempt to understand their predicament in a futile but dogged manner. Like many of Feingold's installations since 1990, the humor of the pseudological (and slightly erotic) *If/Then* only incompletely masks its trenchant critique of the technologically saturated future that is now emerging.

Matthew Biro

other recent works, the artist says, "Conversations are generated in real time, utilizing speech recognition, natural language processing, conversation/personality algorithms, and text-to-speech software." Behind the head, the viewer may read the text produced by the head's speech-recognition software, as well as the responses generated by its conversation algorithms. The head's conversations, one soon discovers, are inevitably inane. Not only does it consistently misrecognize words, but its algorithms compel it to ask extremely philosophical questions that emphasize the absurdity of its responses. Sometimes it seems to respond to something we have said, at other times it seems prerecorded, and occasionally it spontaneously breaks down into nonsensical and childish rhyming. As computer-machine complexes come to life in Feingold's art, they suggest a dysfunctional and pathetic existence, a form of cybernetic life that struggles to understand the reality of its existence but cannot, due to the paucity of its powers of reasoning and imagination.

Ken Feingold

Ken Feingold

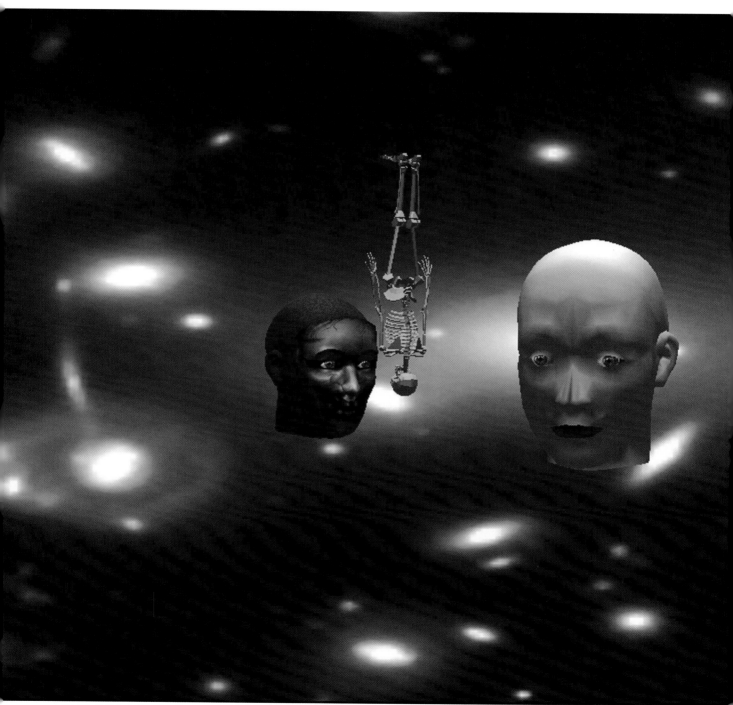

fig. 29 *Self Portrait as the Center of the Universe* (detail), 2001, multimedia installation, 68 x 36 x 36", installation dimensions with projection variable.
Courtesy Postmasters Gallery, New York

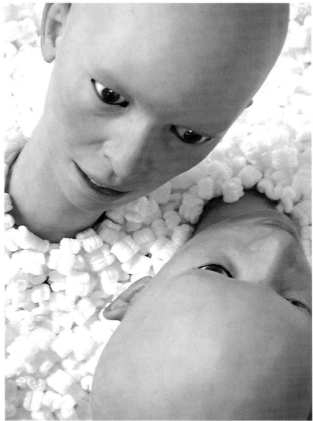

fig. 30 *If/Then*, 2001, multimedia installation, 24 x 24 x 28". Collection of Anne Hoger and Robert Conn, Del Mar, Calif.

Kojo Griffin

- b. 1971, Farmville, Va.
- lives and works in Atlanta
- 3 paintings, 1 collage, and 4 drawings
- gallery 24

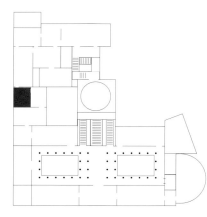

Kojo Griffin's sometimes adorable, frequently evil menagerie illuminates the dark corners of the world with which we are all familiar. Anthropomorphized elephants, bears, birds, and horses team up with depictions of crudely stitched, Frankensteinish children's toys in a veritable litany of disturbing incidents, bad behavior, questionable motives, and evil intent. Griffin's clean, modern palette belies the lonely, heartbreaking, and violent subject matter depicted in his paintings, collages, and drawings. Each work presents a still of some pivotal moment within a larger, unknown narrative—the precarious climax when danger and destruction seem imminent yet not certain.

The cast in Griffin's works, despite appearances, seems entirely, plausibly human—arguing, riding bicycles, smoking, having sex, and prone to sudden bursts of despair and senseless violence. They even have the rare transcendent moment. The artist has said that he substitutes animals for people to inoculate his works from the associations of race, nationality, religion, ethnicity, sexual orientation, social class, and occasionally gender. This is animal husbandry with bite; Griffin's fig-ures stand in as surrogates for our own painful fears of victimization and loss.

Griffin's attraction to his themes arises from his fascination with the tangled kinks of the human psyche. He graduated from Morehouse College in Atlanta with a psychology degree, planning to become a child psychologist. But a long-standing interest in art intervened, and he began showing his work in group exhibitions, which led to his inclusion in both the *2000 Whitney Biennial* and *Freestyle*, organized in 2001 by the Studio Museum in Harlem.

The flat backgrounds of Griffin's works are typically divided into geometric fields of color strewn with loosely drawn and painted symbols and patterns. The oversized scale and contrasting motifs—DNA helixes, chemical diagrams, interlocking rings or cells, printed circuits, blossoms and vines, designs from the Cabala and the I Ching—seem to evoke the underlying systems of interaction and the conflicts of the characters that populate each work. Nature versus nurture, science versus religion, morality versus society. Griffin's perpetrators and victims act out their roles surrounded by symbols that bring to mind the long history of questions and explanations embedded in the various actions depicted. Are we hard-wired for cruelty, or is victimhood learned? Is our own biology the solution, or the problem? Can we understand our own actions, or are we simply one of Griffin's anthropomorphic figures, controlled by complex forces we can no more understand than control? No easy answers are provided, but the complex and painterly layering of subjects, symbols, colors, and shapes adds shades of meaning and interpretation that make Griffin's pictures effective, if unnerving, windows into the evildoing of human beings.

One of the artist's largest paintings to date, *Untitled (man handing candy to girl)* (2001; fig. 34), shows an elephant-man bending over, his arm extended to offer some candy to the small bear-girl in the foreground. She reaches for the wrapped treats in his palm, as her male companion attempts to tug her away. A strong tension is created by the narrow gap between the hand of the would-be victimizer and that of the could-be victim, and the ultimate outcome is unclear. However, the background of gears overlaid with repetitive circuits seems to imply an almost mechanically structured precision to this encounter. Candy is offered, it is taken, or not, and another victim is found, or escapes with naiveté intact. The cloud-filled sky universalizes the encounter; it could be taking place anywhere, to anyone, yesterday, today, or tomorrow.

In the work on paper *Untitled (man with letter, woman standing)* (2001; fig. 31), Griffin presents a more ambiguous scene. The working-class horse-man, downcast, listens as his bird-wife expresses her disappointment at something he has done or that has been done to him. The sheet of paper in his hand could be an eviction notice, an unpaid bill, or a pink slip—in any event, probably not good news for a couple expecting a baby. The background of tangled vines appears indicative of their inextricably entwined lives, their problems gone to seed, constricting and overgrown. Instead of evoking childhood fears, this work presents the intricacies of adulthood, fraught with disappointments, tension, and shame.

Untitled (man with girl) (2002; fig. 35) shows a young horse-woman being undressed by a seated older male creature. Her hunched posture, depressed look, and limp arms bespeak her extreme sense of humility—perhaps she is resigned or helpless in the hands of the perpetrator. The bed nearby leaves it up to the viewer to

fig. 31 *Untitled (man with letter, woman standing)*, 2001, acrylic, collage, charcoal, and graphite on paper, 23 3/4 x 20 1/8". Private Collection, Courtesy Mitchell-Innes & Nash, New York

interpret this distressing narrative. Perhaps the man is not a perpetrator at all but actually the caretaker of a disabled girl, who is unable to perform the simple task of dressing herself.

Griffin has also produced a number of charcoal drawings. Some are preparatory studies for larger works in color, while others appear to be stand-alone pieces. Unlike his paintings, the drawings have no backgrounds and are spare in composition and line, with little or no modeling. This minimal visual vocabulary, especially the lack of color, provides a much quieter, private counterpoint to the seemingly more public action taking place in the paintings. Griffin's talents as a draftsman are on display here, and it is that talent—his skilled line work and carefully crafted composition—that is at the core of his potent evocation of the vulnerability we all share.

Stacey Schmidt

Kojo Griffin

fig. 32 *Untitled,* 2002, charcoal on paper, 22 ¹/₂ x 25 ¹/₄". Courtesy Saltworks Gallery, Atlanta

fig. 33 *Untitled,* 2002, charcoal on paper, 20 x 22 ¹/₂". Courtesy Saltworks Gallery, Atlanta

fig. 34 *Untitled (man handing candy to girl)*, 2001, acrylic, collage, charcoal, and graphite on wood panel, 95 ³/₄ x 119 ⁵/₈". Private Collection

Kojo Griffin

fig. 35 *Untitled (man with girl)*, 2002, acrylic, collage, charcoal, and graphite on wood panel, 48 x 60". Partial and promised gift of P. Bruce Marine and Donald Hardy

fig. 36 *Untitled (man helpin' man up, man walking toward)*, 2002, acrylic, collage, charcoal, and graphite on wood panel, 71 ⁷/₈ x 88 ⁷/₈".
P. Bruce Marine and Donald Hardy Collection

Tim Hawkinson

- b. 1960, San Francisco
- lives and works in Los Angeles
- 1 sculptural installation
- gallery 29

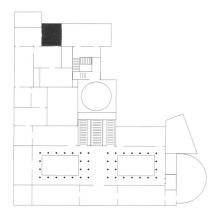

Tim Hawkinson has become, in a brief span of time, one of today's most innovative sculptors, wrestling with questions of human identity in the context of our rapidly changing, technology-driven society. Hawkinson studied in the 1980s at San Jose State University and the University of California, Los Angeles, where he was influenced by the conceptual sculptural practices of Bruce Nauman and Chris Burden focusing on the body and technology. Eschewing the performance and video activities that Burden and Nauman also employed, Hawkinson concentrated, with a singular drive and intensity, on the creation of two- and three-dimensional works throughout the 1990s. His drawings, photographs, sculptures, and installations, most of which blur the distinctions that separate these different media, reveal a densely interconnected formal and thematic richness that has few rivals today.

At the heart of Hawkinson's creative practices over the past fifteen years is an extended meditation on the increasingly cybernetic nature of our society—an examination of the fact that, as the rapid globalization of the world continues to develop, human beings have become ever more densely interconnected through multiple forms of technology. This focus, which finds its historical roots in the (proto-dada) conceptual art of Marcel Duchamp, is given tremendous new life in Hawkinson's work, which generally succeeds at being simultaneously humorous, poignant, and profound. Like Duchamp, Hawkinson uses technology and techniques of measurement to break down the human body—most often his own—thereby rendering it more abstract. He demonstrates how easily the organic may interface with the mechanical, and how quickly both may be transformed. Much more than Duchamp, however, Hawkinson evokes a world existing well beyond the human realm by creating cyborgs, strange hybrid organisms that suggest linkages between human beings, animals, and machines.

Numerous forms of cyborgs populate Hawkinson's art. One of his earliest works, *Untitled (Chicken)* (1986), for example, is a varnished chicken skin stretched on a wire frame, its wings extended. Suggesting a half-organic, half-metal airship, it offers an evocative critique of the mechanization of agriculture. To create the "Blindspot" series (1991–95), Hawkinson photographed every part

fig. 37 *Drip* (detail; unfinished state), 2002. Courtesy the artist and Ace Gallery, Los Angeles

of his body that was inaccessible to his own vision. By assembling a photographically produced "map" of his "blind spots," Hawkinson came up with a strange fishlike form that he reproduced serially in different media. Through the process by which it was made, this half-human, half-animal shape suggests that we can never fully know ourselves, and it also implies the artist's own potential deformation or devolution as the result of technological manipulation. Technology, as these works suggest, affects human development in profound yet unpredictable ways. In works such as *Signature* (1993), *Penitent* (1994), *Tuva* (1995), and *Pentecost* (1999), rudimentary and mechanically articulated humanoid forms, composed of scavenged trash and cheap, mass-produced materials such as cardboard, are configured to simulate complex human activities, for example, writing and making music. These figures, which break down distinctions between animate and inanimate, human and machine, process and finished state, underline the instability of traditional definitions of humankind.

Despite, or perhaps because of, his cybernetic subject matter, Hawkinson is not afraid to tackle elemental themes and myths, content that he often introduces through the materials used to construct his heterogeneous works. Flowing air, for example, with all its connotations of breath and spirit, has been a central element in Hawkinson's work since the early 1990s. Used in conjunction with pumps and compressors, ducts and tubing, and other structuring materials such as latex, vinyl, and woven polyethylene, air was first employed by Hawkinson to animate three-dimensional reproductions of his own nude body—goofy avatars that were usually suspended from the ceiling like balloons. This insubstantial material soon took on a much more complex function in Hawkinson's increasingly large and abstract environmental sculptures, including *Bagpipe* (1995), the interconnected *Head and Reservoir* (both 1995), and the monumental *Überorgan* (2000). Now used in conjunction with computers, sensors, music programs, and sound-making devices, air has become a medium through which Hawkinson's works have begun to make a crude form of music and thereby address their audiences. Like his earlier humanoid cyborgs (some of which also employed flowing air), these large-scale pneumatic cyborgs confound distinctions between living and dead, organic and inorganic. Even more than the humanoids, these air-driven, mechanized hybrids undermine boundaries between human and animal, as well as between the individual and the collective. As we gaze upon what are now often interconnected forms spanning multiple rooms, it is unclear whether we are looking at a single entity or a colony.

Hawkinson's most recent environmental sculpture, *Drip* (2002), commissioned for the 47th Biennial, marks the artist's turn to the elemental material water, the origin of life on this planet. *Drip* is essentially a water-recycling system. Large tentacles drip water into buckets, while a central water-control mechanism uses random input to help generate rhythmic patterns in the falling drops. Like Hawkinson's pneumatic cyborgs, this large-scale cyborg erases traditional distinctions between humans, animals, and machines, mixing organic and industrial materials to fabricate a creature that simulates communication and the making of art. Even more than his air-driven creatures, the water cyborg suggests the conflation of the most advanced with the most primitive. As Hawkinson's art suggests, it is a strange new world that we live in, one in which each evolutionary step forward reveals forgotten elements of a primordial past.

Matthew Biro

Tim Hawkinson

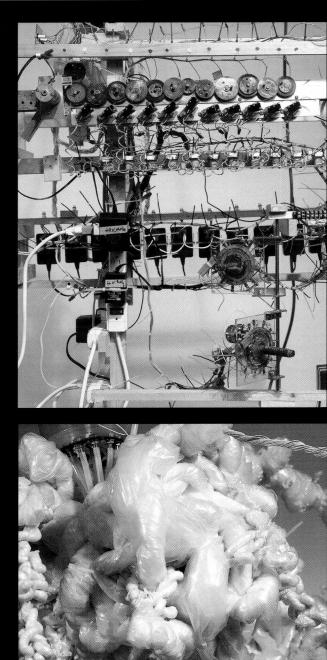

figs. 38-39 *Drip* (detail; unfinished state), 2002. Courtesy the artist and Ace Gallery, Los Angeles

fig. 40 *Drip* (unfinished state), 2002, polyethylene, vinyl, aluminum, mechanical components, and water, 10 x 12 x 15', installation dimensions variable. Courtesy the artist and Ace Gallery, Los Angeles

Bruce Nauman

- b. 1941, Fort Wayne, Ind.
- lives and works in Galisteo, N.M.
- 1 seven-projection video installation
- gallery 14

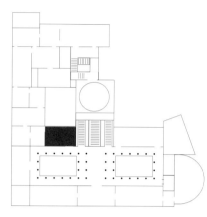

The vision of the great artist working in his isolated studio is a long-standing trope in traditional histories of art—that the artist was a "he" was taken for granted by these histories. The studio was where the artist could contemplate, concentrate, and create, free from the distractions of ordinary life. The fruit of such seclusion, according to this romantic myth, was the masterpiece, whose transcendent quality had been nourished by the otherworldly mystery of the studio, the artist's inner sanctum.

Bruce Nauman, one of the most influential and controversial artists of our time, has a less exalted vision of the studio, essentially demystifying what goes on there. A studio is simply where an artist does what he does, and Nauman has made an aesthetic out of the experience. His most recent series, "Mapping the Studio (Fat Chance John Cage)," is a signature example and may represent a new pinnacle of achievement. However, Nauman's thinking on this subject dates back to at least 1968 and the early videos *Slow Angle Walk (Beckett Walk)* and *Wall-Floor Positions*, which show the artist in his workspace engaging in systematic yet awkward behavior. Unlike anything previously seen in the context

of art, the imagery is nonetheless straightforward and unexceptional. In one video he walks with stiff limbs. In the other he adopts a series of poses in relation to the wall and floor, holding each pose for about forty-five seconds. Nauman's vision of the studio is more strange than mysterious. For the viewer, this often results in an inability to rationalize the obvious.

Nauman began working on his latest project, "Mapping the Studio," in the summer of 2000 by videotaping his studio at night. With a standard video camera, forty-two one-hour videocassettes, and infrared light, he proceeded to record the goings-on in seven locations within his workplace. Before going to bed at night, he turned on the camera, which recorded a single location for the duration of the videocassette. Each site was recorded over a period of six nights. In *Mapping the Studio I (Fat Chance John Cage)*, the first seven-projection installation of the series (corresponding to the seven locations), the raw footage was edited together to produce a stunningly empty, trance-inducing nocturnal adventure in an eerie night-vision green. With an epic duration of almost six hours, during which very little—

72   The 47th Corcoran Biennial

fig. 41 *Mapping the Studio II with color shift, flip, flop & flip/flop (Fat Chance John Cage) All Action Edit* (detail), 2001, 7 DVDs, 7 DVD players, 7 digital projectors, 7 pairs of speakers, 10 x 12' images, installation dimensions variable. Collection Walker Art Center, Minneapolis, T. B. Walker Acquisition Fund, 2002. View of installation at Sperone Westwater Gallery, New York

and some might argue nothing at all—actually happens, a viewer searches eagerly for the sights and sounds of anything capable of marking time, from the scurrying of mice along the floor to the rushing wind outside.

Nauman demonstrates his abiding investigative drive in this study of the place that is home to his creative expression. Yet the project also implies an element of frustration. Nauman is well known for his recurring bouts of artist's block, and he had not produced a major work in four years when he began developing "Mapping the Studio." In this series he seems to have turned the camera on his inactivity. He examines the disused corners, remnants of past activity, works in progress, and the general detritus of his studio as if closely analyzing these things were a way to apply pressure to the situation, to force a change and discover a way beyond the impasse. Life alone in his rural New Mexico studio is, for Nauman, what the proverbial blank page is for the writer. In this case, he faces the ongoing challenge by using it as fodder for his art. He videotaped the space of his unproductiveness, the lack of a defined subject being an empty metaphor, one might say, for the formidable task that all artists face.

In addition to the original version, there are three others that, together, complete the series of seven-channel works.[1] *Mapping the Studio II with color shift, flip, flop & flip/flop (Fat Chance John Cage)* shows the original footage manipulated with image flips (left to right or vice versa), flops (top to bottom or vice versa), combinations of the two (flips and flops), and color shifts. These formal transformations, in offbeat video-tinged hues ranging from red to green to blue, add a sickly dimension to the already unsettling experience. The final two versions, called "All Action Edits," are pared-down versions of *Mapping the Studio I* and *II* that show only the so-called action.

Mapping the Studio II with color shift, flip, flop & flip/flop (Fat Chance John Cage) All Action Edit (2001), the version featured in *Fantasy Underfoot*, is the most eye-popping of the foursome. When watching either of the two unedited versions, one has to be patient and pay close attention to see, for example, moths flitting and legging the wire mesh of the screen door, or canny mice successfully avoiding Toonsis, the cat that is the sometimes scheming, sometimes bored predator-protagonist. Often there is little more than a

Bruce Nauman

moment before the "action" disappears. The situation is very different in the present all action edit, which inundates the viewer with dizzying highlights. The self-examination suggested by the meditative unedited versions is transformed into a skittish mood of surveillance where the cat meows, mice evade, coyotes howl, horses neigh, wind blows, rain falls, moths fly, and so on, all the time.

The lesson is Cagean in nature, a point noted by the subtitle of the series, which refers to the renowned composer and philosopher whose interest in Zen Buddhism and process led to the decision to remove intention from his music. Cage accorded sound and noise equal status and regarded silence as an entity in its own right. Like Cage, Nauman shows us how content is everywhere and indistinguishable from everything else. What we perceive as discrete subject matter is, more accurately, a highly focused lens through which we view only the tiniest aspect of the perceivable world. Nauman introduces personal value into this trenchant Cagean model. "Mapping the Studio" is a portrait of the private life of the artist, made, for the most part, in his absence. A mesmerizing, vertiginous, and telescopic view of virtually nothing, it is among Nauman's most intimate and ironically revealing works to date.

Audiences now have the opportunity to enter the studio of an artist as famously reclusive as Andy Warhol was sociable. But just as we enter, he exits . . . repeatedly. Over and over again Nauman crosses the path of the camera, heading out for the night, the heels of his cowboy boots rhythmically clicking on the floor, the screen door slamming behind him. Part self-effacement and part dismissive of the space itself, the implication may be that more action awaits both the artist and the viewer outside the inner sanctum of the vaunted artist's studio. The point is underscored by the fascinating, and sometimes slightly scary, sounds that invade the space from the outside. These sounds suggest the natural order of things, a miracle that is equally enacted inside, but on a smaller scale. Contrary to the traditional myths of art history, what separates the romance of the studio from everything else is, in Nauman's vision, porous. Despite this, he has succeeded in transforming this natural order into an experience that is entirely unlike any other. Nauman shows us a studio whose mystery is similar to that which characterizes the rest of the world. However, what may be most remarkable is his ability to show us the mystery at all.

Jonathan P. Binstock

1. In addition to the four seven-projection installations, there are two related single-channel works: *Office Edit I (Fat Chance John Cage) Mapping the Studio* and *Office Edit II with color shift, flip, flop & flip/flop (Fat Chance John Cage) Mapping the Studio*, both 2001. These show only the desk in the empty studio office.

fig. 42 Video still from *Mapping the Studio II with color shift, flip, flop & flip/flop (Fat Chance John Cage) All Action Edit*, 2001. Collection Walker Art Center, Minneapolis, T. B. Walker Acquisition Fund, 2002, Courtesy Sperone Westwater Gallery, New York

Bruce Nauman

Bruce Nauman

fig. 43 Video stills from *Mapping the Studio II with color shift, flip, flop & flip/flop (Fat Chance John Cage) All Action Edit,* 2001. Collection Walker Art Center, Minneapolis, T. B. Walker Acquisition Fund, 2002, Courtesy Sperone Westwater Gallery, New York

Nigel Poor

• b. 1963, Boston
• lives and works in San Francisco
• 216 photographs
• the rotunda

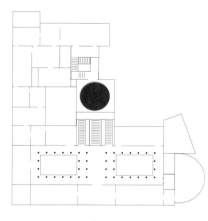

Since 1998, photographer Nigel Poor has worked on a succession of large-scale projects with sociological overtones. She began each one by detailing a set of instructions for actions, which were then systematically executed. A given project may take as many as three years to complete, allowing ample time for the artist to alter the plans as her research unfolds, based upon her changing vision and ideas about the work's eventual installation. Nonetheless, once a project has been initiated, its premise and basic framework cannot be altered. Poor is like a social scientist. The final presentation of a given work may take many forms, but to change its generative hypothesis is likely to alter the enterprise in its entirety.

Poor's latest body of work, *Three Objects* (2002), is, according to the artist's working statement, "an investigation of the diminishing chains of connection between people." When she initiated research for the piece, her instructions were more or less as follows: Ask an individual to participate in the uneasy task of self-description by choosing three objects that characterize him or her well. Then ask this person to name another individual, to whom the artist will then pose the same question. Also ask this second individual to choose three more objects, these describing the person who directed the artist to the present individual. Follow this process and create a diminishing chain of connection between thirteen people. To create a sense of closure, the thirteenth subject will be asked only to offer three objects describing the twelfth subject. Complete the entire process three times to produce three diminishing chains of connection.

Poor began the research for the first chain in San Francisco, where she lives and works. The other two chains were started in New Brunswick, Maine, while she was on a fellowship at Bowdoin College's Coastal Studies Center. Each participant in the finished chains is represented by a framed set of six photographs, or a "pod," as the artist has referred to the sets, and each pod is accompanied by a label giving that person's age, sex, and occupation. The first pod, representing the first San Francisco subject—thirty-five, female, a teacher— shows the three objects she chose to describe herself. A worn blanket, an egg-shaped tchotchke, and a photo assemblage are pictured against a black monochromatic background, the top row of a 3-by-2 grid of images (fig. 45). The bottom three photos show the objects selected by the second participant to describe the first: a toy house, a bag of candy, and another blanket, this one crocheted. These images have a white background. And so goes the diminishing chain, from the first pod, which has the largest images, each measuring 11 by 11 inches, to the twelfth and smallest pod, with images measuring $5^1/2$ by $5^1/2$ inches. Graphically designed elements affixed to the walls around the pods further suggest how to interpret the layout, which resembles a kind of family tree.

Though Poor never formally defines hypotheses for her research, she often develops her projects based upon certain ideas about what she might learn when they are finally completed. In *Three Objects*, her initial questions are implied by the structure of the finished product: Can the deep personal value a person ascribes to one of his or her possessions be conveyed through a photograph of that object, and, if so, does the fact that people are connected to one another indirectly, through mutual acquaintances, reveal itself in the objects they choose to describe themselves?

The images in the first pod of the San Francisco chain convincingly suggest a close relationship between the first two participants. The crocheted blanket selected by the second person clearly indicates specific knowledge of the teacher's worn blanket, which may be a remnant from her childhood. The photograph assemblage of loved ones in the top row and the toy house in the bottom row indicate a different kind of connection: an awareness of the importance of family, close-knit bonds, and "home" in the teacher's life.

Poor's reasoning may seem logical enough, and obvious links like these appear in pods throughout the chains. But to interpret her study as scientific in nature would, of course, be a mistake. Nonetheless, despite the uncontrolled quality of her investigation, the collection of imagery reveals much about how people understand one another through material objects, and what they share through common cultural contexts. For example, every pod in the San Francisco group has at least one kitsch knickknack. And the third chain—the second one done in Maine—ends with six women, all of whose pods include objects with spiritual connotations, such as reassuring words or aphorisms. One pod has an

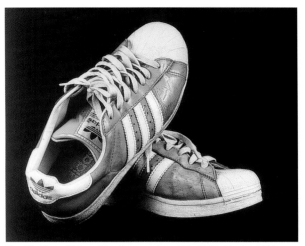

fig. 44 *Three Objects* (detail; group 1, pod 2), 2002, C-print, $10^1/2$ x $10^1/2$". Courtesy the artist and Haines Gallery, San Francisco, with the support of the Coastal Studies Center, Bowdoin College, Brunswick, Maine

image of an angel figurine holding above its head a card with the word "healing," another a stone with the word "faith," and another a rosary. The links are evident, but what they signify is open to interpretation.

Perhaps the most provocative connections are the ones most difficult to account for, those that seem to transcend the influence of social networks. In pod two of the San Francisco chain, four of the six photographs—the sneakers, a Seattle Space Needle snow globe, a portrait of the late comedian Chris Farley, and the glue pen—have a similar high-keyed, light blue hue. Is this a coincidence, or does the recurrence accurately point to that individual's preference for the color? Sometimes Poor's compositional decisions and grid layouts underscore these seemingly coincidental links and embellish their significance, such as in the repeating vertical forms of the Space Needle and glue stick in the central photos of this pod. Formal associations like these owe as much to the actual objects as to Poor's approach to still-life photography, which makes her ordinary subjects seem distinctive through eccentric distortions of scale and a remarkably precise imaging technique. Her strict control over the medium, zealous attention to detail, and immaculate artificial backdrops give emphasis to the faux science that characterizes her work. But these aspects also cultivate an expansive sensation of fantasy. Her project tells stories and inspires interpretations that, while based on reality, are entirely invented. Poor's signature ability is to make virtually anything seem beautiful, to create provocative narratives where none would seem to exist, and, in effect, to find freedom through discipline and the unique rigor of her craft.

Jonathan P. Binstock

Nigel Poor

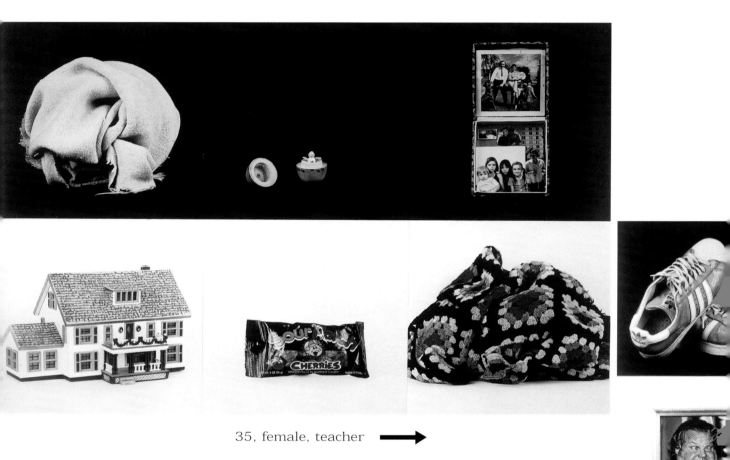

35, female, teacher ➡

fig. 45 *Three Objects* (detail; group 1, pods 1–3), 2002, 216 C-prints, size ranging from 11 x 11" to 5 1/2 x 5 1/2". Courtesy the artist and Haines Gallery, San Francisco, with the support of the Coastal Studies Center, Bowdoin College, Brunswick, Maine

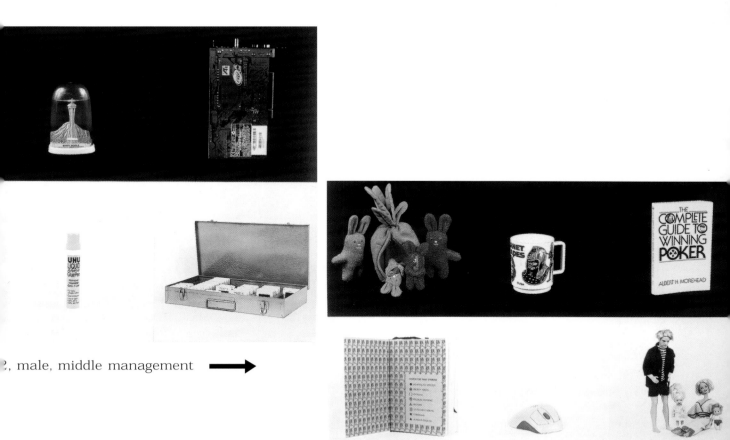

2, male, middle management ➡

33, male, art director ➡

Susan Smith-Pinelo

- b. 1969, Duxbury, Mass.
- lives and works in Washington, D.C.
- 3 sculptural video installations
- gallery 21

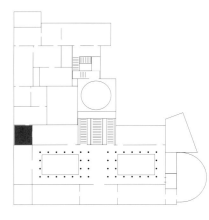

Susan Smith-Pinelo's video installations for the Corcoran Biennial grew out of her uneasy love affair with the world of hip-hop. Hers is an on-again, off-again romance that has balanced an attraction to the rhythms and rhymes of rap on MTV with a repugnance for the violence and misogyny of the genre. As a thirty-something feminist, Smith-Pinelo creates artworks that yank debates about identity out of the political and social realms and place them firmly in the personal. *Dances with Hip Hop* (2000; fig. 46), *Asstronomical Proportions I* (from the *Hiphopcrisy* series) (2002; fig. 47), and *Asstronomical Proportions II* (from the *Hiphopcrisy* series) (2002; fig.48) force us to consider the artist's complex position on contemporary female identity, which is filtered through her contradictory feelings about the hormone-fueled "gangsta" fantasies of hip-hop.

Upon entering the gallery, one encounters the three suspended monitors of *Dances with Hip Hop* in the center of the room. The three stacked televisions that make up the work are suspended from the ceiling by wired hardware. To the left and right of this are *Asstronomical Proportions I* and *Asstronomical*

Proportions II, each consisting of a grouping of monitors atop tall, mirror-covered, semicircular platforms that reference any strip club. The upper monitor of *Dances with Hip Hop* shows the artist's head intently grooving to a silent beat, while the middle and bottom monitors display, respectively, the bra-clad torso and the panty-covered hips of two other women, also dancing silently. The artist's head seems lost in a kind of private reverie—eyes gazing at nothing or closed, face turned slightly away from the viewer's gaze, glancing at the lens from time to time—lost in the rhythm of the song. The other monitors show fetishized body parts in a clear public display. The breasts are caressed and jiggled, the hips sway and thrust, both directly confronting the viewer. While the head is unaware of what the body is doing, the composite figure ultimately seems somewhat cohesive, as if the body parts are independently performing learned movements specific to hip-hop beats. The monitors each cut and jump in a kind of disjointed order, but when all three dancers unexpectedly pause at the same break, or all move toward one side of the screen, the figure suddenly gels as a whole. Smith-Pinelo purposefully breaks down the female body to highlight those parts most fetishized in hip-hop videos. These parts of the body literally become "equipment," as their substance and weight are conveyed through the sculptural forms of the monitors. The video reveals an inherent conflict in Smith-Pinelo's views on this objectification, as her closed eyes and hypnotic moves clearly reveal her infatuation with the music.

In *Asstronomical Proportions I* and *Asstronomical Proportions II,* Smith-Pinelo further deconstructs the black woman's body by zeroing in on the twin coins of the hip-hop realm—the crotch and the booty. In *Asstronomical Proportions I,* Smith-Pinelo gives us a cropped clip of a dancer's lycra-covered bottom rapidly shaking and bouncing as she boogies to the still-unheard beat. The lack of music focuses attention on the repetition of the movements, patterns that are enhanced by the synchronicity of the same image on all three monitors. The closely related *Asstronomical Proportions II* offers up a squatting woman in high-heels, shown opening and closing her strong legs to reveal her thinly veiled crotch. She then stands up, stoops, and the open and closed movement is repeated. The movements are slow and concentrated, and the viewer encountering these works becomes a willing spectator of the entertainment, or even a participant in it. As with any stimulus, repeated exposure quickly desensitizes the audience, yet encountering these images in the safe confines of a museum is disconcerting.

In both *Asstronomical Proportions I* and *II,* Smith-Pinelo presents women's body parts as abstracted fragments standing in for all the forms of vicarious fantasy consumption that populate hip-hop and rap videos. She is particularly intrigued with how this fictive portrayal of the good life butts heads with the real lifestyles of both the performers and their audience. The fancy cars, guns, furs, jewelry, and thug life seen in typical hip-hop videos are little more than rented window dressing and playacting. Smith-Pinelo simultaneously celebrates and critiques this language of hip-hop as both an informed viewer and a willing participant. In highlighting hip-hop's degrading yet seductive fetishism of women and her reaction to it, she strips away the veneer of the genre's dearly held fantasies. Yet these fantasies, as she perceptively points out, have a power and pull that transcend reality and keep her going back for more.

Stacey Schmidt

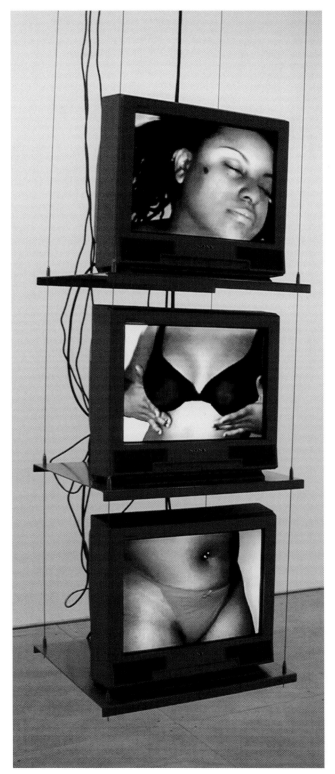

fig. 46 *Dances with Hip Hop*, 2000, 3 DVDs, 3 DVD players, and 3 monitors, installation dimensions variable. Courtesy Fusebox, Washington, D.C.

Susan Smith-Pinelo

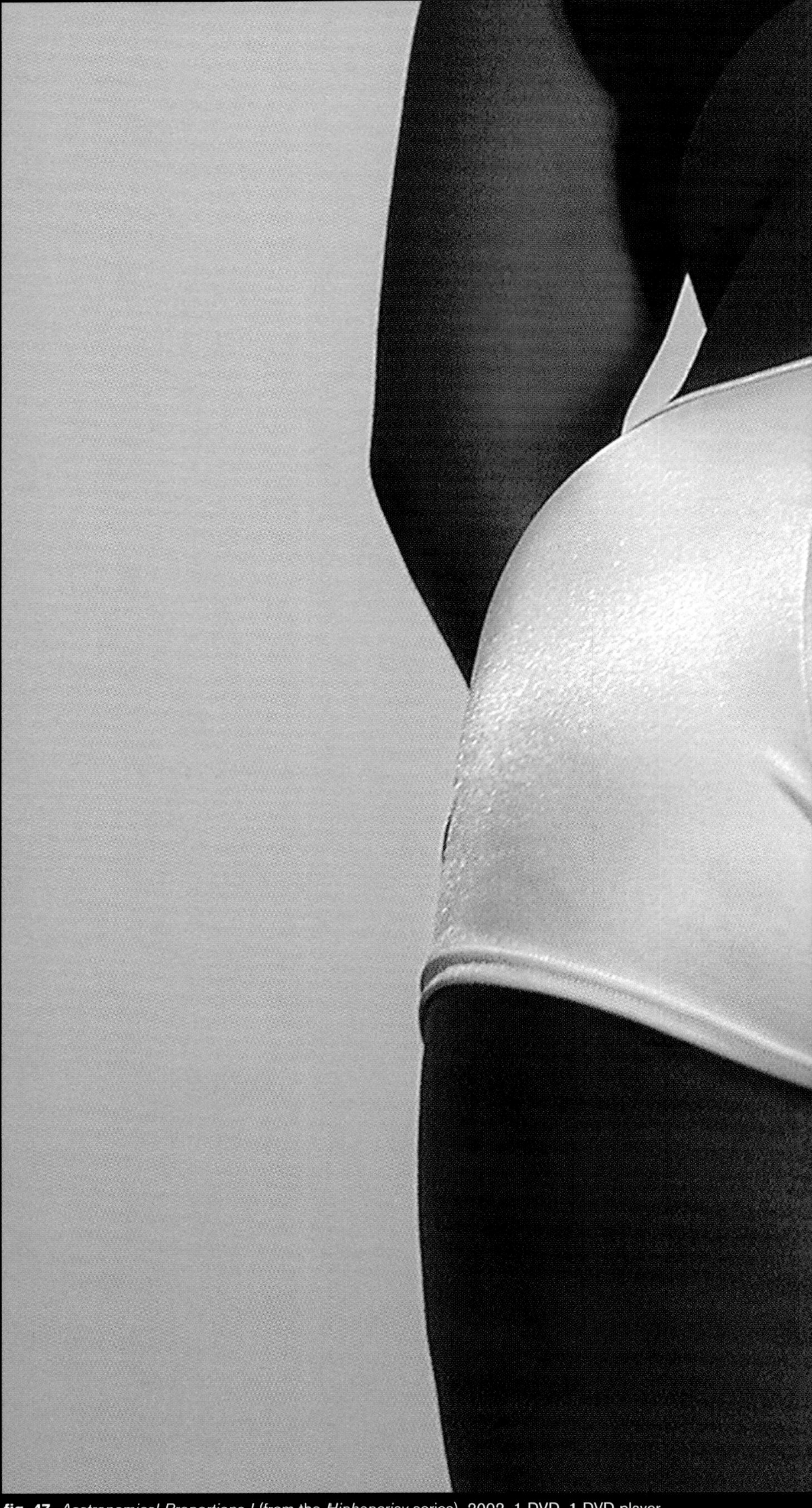

fig. 47 *Asstronomical Proportions I* (from the *Hiphopcrisy* series), 2002, 1 DVD, 1 DVD player, and 3 monitors, installation dimensions variable. Courtesy Fusebox, Washington, D.C.

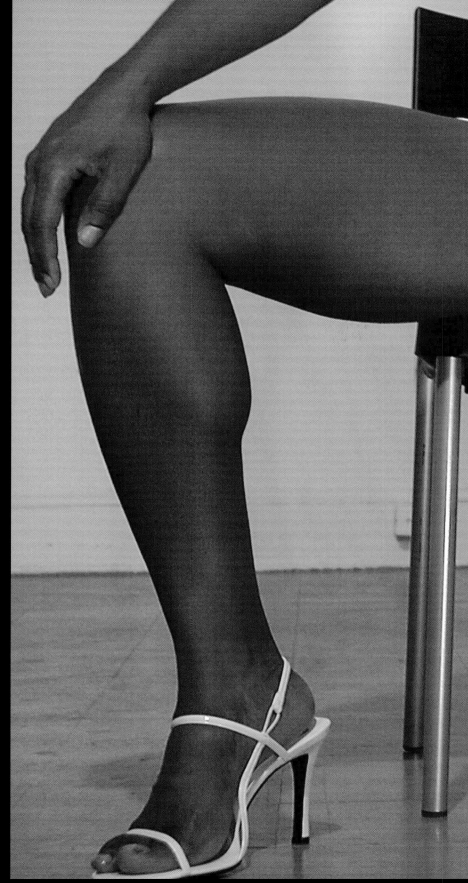

fig. 48 *Asstronomical Proportions II* (from the *Hiphopcrisy* series), 2002, 1 DVD, 1 DVD player, and 3 monitors, installation dimensions variable. Courtesy Fusebox, Washington, D.C.

Bruce Yonemoto

- b. 1949, San Jose, Calif.
- lives and works in Los Angeles
- sculpture. video, video installation, and 4 photographs
- gallery 2€

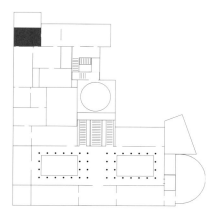

Bruce Yonemoto's set of three related installations is centered on ideas of globalism and desire. Buckminster Fuller's 1969 text *Operating Manual for Spaceship Earth* is the unseen touchstone for the diverse elements in these complex displays that suggest a wide range of associations, from global connectedness and international commerce to 1960s ideas of masculinity.

Fuller's concept of "Spaceship Earth"—as humanity's mobile home traveling through the universe—is, for Yonemoto, best represented by a desktop globe. Appearing in several elements of the installation, the globe reminds us of the simple yet profound fact—which Fuller also wanted us to remember—that the world we live in is a physical object that we share as humans. However, for Yonemoto, the traditional globe also has a negative implication. While showing the world in its totality, the globe also reveals a world divided into political units, presenting a picture of both global unity and divisiveness. The depiction of sovereign states implies that national differences supersede all other differences as well as any commonalities.

In *Top of the World*, a collection of over a dozen vintage globes rests on top of each of two semicircular tables with an inset bar displaying bottles of liquor from around the world. The implication is that alcohol gives the drinker a sense of escaping from the world, of being on top of it. Theoretically, this sense of seeing the world from the outside is the only perspective from which to view it clearly in its entirety. But the drinker discovers, paradoxically, that being on top of the world is, in fact, the most distorted vantage point of all. Or perhaps a drinker's tendency to blur distinctions suggests the actual condition of the world, one in which complex interdependencies and sociopolitical and economic affiliations blur the supposedly neat boundaries between states.

The well-stocked bar also seems to call to mind the international man of leisure—the playboy. If Hugh Hefner can be considered the archetype, and Austin Powers his parodic successor, then the figure of the playboy truly belongs to the 1960s. Masculinity was then still bolstered, not undermined, by the display of pleasure-seeking sophistication. Was the global orientation of the playboy a sign of growing commonality, or did it simply support a regime of masculine self-aggrandizement? The artist gives no sign of passing judgment on this now-outdated image of masculinity, perhaps offering it as a nostalgic counterpoint to the present-day near ubiquity of "family values."

In another part of the installation, four globes sit on pedestals. Inside three of the globes, films are shown on tiny monitors visible through peepholes. In one, the film *Journey to the Center of the Earth*, based on the novel written in 1864 by French author Jules Verne, reinforces the physicality of the planet Earth by picturing the act of traveling through it. This geophysical sense of the planet is reinforced by NASA footage screened inside a second globe. The third presents the 1960 sci-fi classic *The Time Machine*, based on the novel written in 1895 by H. G. Wells, which, through the use of time-lapse photography and the animation technique known as "claymation," calls attention to the passage of time. These techniques demonstrate that film has its own denotations for time, which are not based on the physical rotation of the Earth around the sun. The fourth globe, emitting the audio "It's a Small World," is covered with stucco. The mid-twentieth-century Italian artist Piero Manzoni claimed that stucco is a transformative material because it enables us to realize our fantasies. Utopian visions of world unity, escapist pleasures of film, and fabulous adventures into outer space or the center of the Earth come together in Yonemoto's globes to create a strong sense of human aspirations and dreams.

The still photographs displayed on the wall around these globes are the most disorienting element in Yonemoto's work. In separate frames, a young man of European descent and a young woman of Asian descent pose as if for a fashion magazine, using a globe as a prop. Though the models are somewhat amateurishly posed and their clothes are not particularly fashionable, they seem to be engaged in selling something. To this end, the globe serves as a prop for the real subject of the photograph, which is the desire for something else—an article of clothing, a vacation package, or a megastore. The same globe that could have represented Fuller's common home of humanity becomes, in these photographs, no more than an object, something essentially replaceable. And if the real subject is desire, then the individual is also essentially replaceable, merely an object. Does humanity today share only the ability to be immersed in a system of capitalist commodification?

In the third part of the installation, a large film projection titled *Panpanorama*, Yonemoto doctors the famous "kiss" scene in Alfred Hitchcock's film *Vertigo*, transforming it into a spectacle of international cinema. Instead of showing the panning shot around the lovers, Yonemoto replaces the background with famous tracking shots from classic international films. Our memory of the original scene stays with us as we watch its replacement. The shared memory of film has a way of uniting us globally; we recognize Jimmy Stewart and Kim Novak in the scene from *Vertigo* as if they were a part of our modern collective unconscious. By doctoring this image, Yonemoto creates a new fantasy for us, in the same way that our imperfect memory alters and merges events from the past. Yonemoto encourages us to enjoy the fantastical recreation. However, by inserting the classic film clips, he is also reminding us that today, fifty years after *Vertigo* was released, the imperial authority of Hollywood is ever increasing its hold on the cinematic world.

Yonemoto has been exploring many of the themes addressed in this exhibition for over twenty-five years. In this installation, he continues to use film both as a metaphor for desire and as a subject in its own right, reminding us that film wields tremendous force in our global culture.

Adam Lerner

Bruce Yonemoto

fig. 49 *Journey to the Center of the Earth*, 2001, globe, DVD player, 2.2" monitor, electrical cord, and monocle, 16 x 12 x 12". Courtesy Blum & Poe, Santa Monica, Calif.

fig. 50 Video stills from *Panpanorama*, 2002, DVD, DVD projector, 12 x 16' image size, installation dimensions variable. Courtesy Blum & Poe, Santa Monica, Calif.

Bruce Yonemoto

figs. 51–54 (left to right) *The Playboy Advisor*, *Atlas*, *Dear Playboy*, and *Playboy After Hours*, all 2002, C-print, 60 x 40". Courtesy Blum & Poe, Santa Monica, Calif., and lemon sky: projects + editions, Los Angeles

Exhibitions and Bibliographies

Linda Besemer

Selected Exhibitions

Solo

2002   Cohan Leslie and Browne, New York

2001   Angles Gallery, Santa Monica, Calif.

Group

2000   *2000 Whitney Biennial*, Whitney Museum of American Art, New York

      Glee, Aldrich Museum of Contemporary Art, Ridgefield, Conn.

1999   *Five Continents and One City: New Paintings from Asia, Europe, North, Central and South America*, Palacio de los Condes de Santiago de Calimaya, Museum of Mexico City

1998   *10 x 20*, Philadelphia Museum of Art

1997   *Examining the Feminine in Contemporary Painting*, Southeastern Center for Contemporary Art (SECCA), Winston-Salem, N.C.

Selected Bibliography

Batchelor, David, and John Yau. *Linda Besemer*. New York and Los Angeles: Cohan Leslie and Browne and Angles Gallery, 2002.

Knight, Christopher. "Catching the Next Wave of Painters." *Los Angeles Times*, 20 June 2000, F1.

Rubinstein, Raphael. "America's Best." *Art in America* (July 2000): 39–40.

Smith, Roberta. "A Profusion of Painting, Very Much Alive." New York Times, 10 May 2002, E31.

Solomon, Deborah. "Tastemaker, New in Town, Dives into a Caldron." *New York Times*, 2 May 2001, 1–9.

Janet Cardiff (and George Bures Miller)

Selected Exhibitions

Solo

2002   Luhring Augustine, New York

2001   *Janet Cardiff: A Survey of Works Including Collaborations with George Bures Miller*, P.S.1 Contemporary Art Center, New York

The Paradise Institute, Canadian Pavilion, *49th Venice Biennale*, Venice, Italy (collaboration with George Bures Miller)

1999   *The Missing Voice (Case Study B)*, Artangel, London

Side Street Projects, Los Angeles

Group

2001   *Elusive Paradise: The Millennium Prize*, National Gallery of Canada, Musée des Beaux-Arts du Canada, Ottawa, Ontario

010101: Art in Technological Times, San Francisco Museum of Modern Art

100 Wishes, Museum Ludwig, Cologne, Germany

2000   *Rumor City—Les rumeurs urbaines/Urban Rumors*, part of *Mutations*, Fri-Art, Centre d'Art Contemporain, Kunsthalle Fribourg, Switzerland

Wonderland, St. Louis Art Museum

1999   *Carnegie International 99/00*, Carnegie Museum of Art, Pittsburgh

Selected Bibliography

Baerwaldt, Wayne, ed. *The Paradise Institute*. Winnipeg, Manitoba, Canada: Plug In Editions, 2001.

Boxer, Sarah. "An Artist Who Travels With You (on Tape, That Is)." *New York Times*, 8 August 2000, E1, E3.

Christov-Bakargiev, Carolyn. Janet Cardiff: A Survey of Works Including Collaborations with George Bures Miller. New York: P.S.1 MOMA, 2001.

Johnson, Ken. "Art in Review: Janet Cardiff and George Bures Miller." New York Times, 12 April 2002, E36.

Nancy Davidson

Selected Exhibitions

Solo

2002 *Plenty*, Regina Gouger Miller Gallery, Carnegie-Mellon University, Pittsburgh

2001 *Crystal Blue Persuasion*, Contemporary Arts Center, Cincinnati

Robert Miller Gallery, New York

1999 *Nancy Davidson: Breathless*, Institute of Contemporary Art, University of Pennsylvania, Philadelphia

nobutsaboutit, Ezra and Cecile Zilkha Gallery, Wesleyan University, Middletown, Conn.

1998 *The Buds and the Beads*, Neuberger Museum, State University of New York, Purchase, N.Y.

Group

2000 *The Living End*, Boulder Museum for Contemporary Art, Boulder, Colo.

1999 *Zero-G: When Gravity Becomes Form*, Whitney Museum of American Art at Champion, Stamford, Conn.

1998 *Pop Surrealism*, Aldrich Museum of Contemporary Art, Ridgefield, Conn.

1997 *SpAces & forms: part II*, Maryland Institute College of Art, Baltimore

1995 *Conceptual Textiles*, John Michael Kohler Arts Center, Sheboygan, Wis.

Selected Bibliography

Johnson, Ken. "Art in Review: Nancy Davidson." *New York Times*, 9 October 1998, E38.

Pachmanova, Martina. *Carnivaleyes*. Prague: Nova Sin Gallery, 1998.

Raczka, Robert. "Nancy Davidson." *Sculpture* 19 (April 2000): 71.

Schaffner, Ingrid. 'Nancy Davidson." In *Pop Surrealism*. Edited by Richard Klein, Dominique Nahas, and Ingrid Schaffner. Ridgefield, Conn.: Aldrich Museum of Contemporary Art, 1998.

Tannenbaum, Judith. *Breathless: Nancy Davidson*. Philadelphia: Institute of Contemporary Art, 1999.

Marcel Dzama

Selected Exhibitions

Solo

2002 John Michael Kohler Arts Center, Sheboygan, Wis.

2001 Richard Heller Gallery, Santa Monica, Calif.

2000 David Zwirner, New York

1998 Art Pace Foundation, San Antonio

Group

2000 *Selections from the Manilow Collection,* Museum of Contemporary Art, Chicago

Drawing Show, Art Institute of Chicago

1998 *Selections Spring '98*, The Drawing Center, New York

Selected Bibliography

Baerwaldt, Wayne, ed. *Marcel Dzama: More Famous Drawings.* Winnipeg, Manitoba, Canada: Plug In Editions, 1999.

Baerwaldt, Wayne, and Marcel Dzama. *Famous Drawings Presents: Marcel Dzama.* Santa Monica, Calif.: Smart Art Press, 1998.

Dzama, Marcel. "Untitled Drawings." *zingmagazine* (Spring-Summer 1999): n.p.

Kimmelman, Michael. "Art in Review: Fantasyland." *New York Times*, 14 June 2002, E38.

McEwen, Adam. "People are strange: Adam McEwen on Marcel Dzama." *Frieze* (May 2001): 66–67.

Pagel, David. "Amiss and Lively." *Los Angeles Times,* 18 July 1997, F24.

Jacob El Hanani

Selected Exhibitions

Solo

2002   Nicole Klagsbrun Gallery, New York

Gallery Joe, Philadelphia

2000   Nicole Klagsbrun Gallery, New York

Gallery Joe, Philadelphia

Mark Moore Gallery, Santa Monica, Calif.

Group

2000   *Morocco: Jews and Art in a Muslim Land*, The Jewish Museum, New York

Collecting Drawings, Not Artists: Gifts from the Collection of Sarah-Ann and Werner H. Kramarsky, Fogg Art Museum, Harvard University, Cambridge, Mass.

Fixations: The Obsessional in Contemporary Art, John Michael Kohler Arts Center, Sheboygan, Wis.

1998   *Edward R. Broida Collection*, Orlando Museum of Art, Orlando, Fla.

Seventies, Tel Aviv Museum, Israel

Artists Using Writing, Wadsworth Atheneum, Hartford

1996   *A Labor of Love*, New Museum of Contemporary Art, New York

Selected Bibliography

Baker, Kenneth. "Jacob El Hanani, Hosfelt Gallery, San Francisco." *Art News* (December 1998): 156.

Boneti, David. "Obsession + Devotion." *San Francisco Examiner*, 24 October 1997, B9.

Danto, Arthur. "Best of 2000." *Artforum* (December 2000): 21.

Johnson, Ken. "Art in Review: Drawings, Nicole Klagsbrun Gallery." *New York Times*, 13 August 1999, E36.

Sozanski, Edward. 'Works that Rely on Invention and Repetition/ 'Drawing Rules' is at Gallery Joe." *Philadelphia Inquirer*, 9 April 1999, 36.

Ken Feingold

Selected Exhibitions

Solo

2001   Postmasters Gallery, New York

1999   Postmasters Gallery, New York

Group

2002   *2002 Whitney Biennial,* Whitney Museum of American Art, New York

Media_city_seoul_2002, Seoul Museum of Art, South Korea

2001   *Devices of Wonder,* J. Paul Getty Museum, Los Angeles

Under the Skin, Wilhelm Lehmbruck Museum, Duisburg, Germany

2000   *Alien Intelligence*, Kiasma Museum of Contemporary Art, Helsinki, Finland

Video Time, Museum of Modern Art, New York

Beware! In Playing the Phantom You Become One, Documenta X, Kassel, Germany

Selected Bibliography

Feingold, Ken. "The Interactive Art Gambit." In *New Screen Media: Cinema/Art/Narrative*. Edited by Martin Rieser and Andrea Zapp. London: British Film Institute, 2001 (includes DVD).

Johnson, Ken. "Art in Review: Ken Feingold." *New York Times*, 26 February 1999, E41.

Morgan, Robert C. "*Un Chien Délicieux* by Ken Feingold (1990)." In *Between Modernism and Conceptual Art*. Edited by Robert C. Morgan. Jefferson, N.C.: McFarland & Co., 1997.

Rush, Michael. *New Media in Late 20th Century Art*. London: Thames and Hudson, 1999.

Wilson, Stephen. *Information Arts: Intersections of Art, Science, Technology*. Cambridge, Mass.: MIT Press, 2001.

Kojo Griffin

Selected Exhibitions

Solo

2003   Museum of Contemporary Art of Georgia, Atlanta

2002   Saltworks Gallery, Atlanta

2001   *Kojo Griffin: Drawings,* The Temporary Contemporary, Cheekwood Museum, Nashville

   Kojo Griffin: New Work, Mitchell-Innes & Nash, New York

   Kojo Griffin, Kemper Museum of Contemporary Art, Kansas City, Mo.

1999   *New Frontiers: Kojo Griffin*, Mint Museum of Art, Charlotte, N.C.

Group

2003   *Splat Boom Pow!: The Influence of Comics in Contemporary Art, 1970–2000*, Contemporary Arts Museum, Houston

2001   *Freestyle,* Studio Museum in Harlem, New York

2000   *2000 Whitney Biennial,* Whitney Museum of American Art, New York

Selected Bibliography

Chambers, Christopher. "Kojo Griffin." *Flash Art* (October 2001): 102–103.

Glueck, Grace. "Art in Review: Kojo Griffin." *New York Times*, 28 September 2001, E38.

Golden, Thelma. *Freestyle*. New York: Studio Museum in Harlem, 2001.

Greenberg Rohatyn, Jeanne. *Super Natural Playground*. Milan: Marella Arte Contemporanea, 2002.

Kimmelman, Michael, "Art in Review: Fantasyland." *New York Times*, 14 June 2002, E38.

Shaw, Louise E. *Georgia Triennial 2002/2003*. Savannah: Telfair Museum of Art, 2002.

Tim Hawkinson

Selected Exhibitions

Solo

2002   *Überorgan*, Ace Gallery, New York

2001   *Directions: Tim Hawkinson*, Hirshhorn Museum and Sculpture Garden, Smithsonian Institution, Washington, D.C.

2000   *Überorgan*, MASS MoCA, North Adams, Mass.

Power Plant, Toronto

Pentecost, Ace Gallery, Los Angeles

Group

2002   *2002 Whitney Biennial*, Whitney Museum of American Art, New York

2001   *The Americans, New Art,* Barbican Gallery, London

Un Art populaire, Fondation Cartier, Paris

2000   *The Greenhouse Effect*, Serpentine Gallery, London

1999   *48th Venice Biennale*, Venice, Italy

Selected Bibliography

Desmarais, Charles. *Humongulous: Sculpture and Other Works by Tim Hawkinson*. Cincinnati: Contemporary Arts Center, 1996.

Gopnik, Blake. "What-If-Ery at Its Purest." *Toronto Globe and Mail*, 22 June 2000, R5.

Harvey, Doug, Philip Monk, and Laura Steward Heon. *Tim Hawkinson*. Toronto: The Power Plant, 2000.

Saltz, Jerry. "Mr. Wizard." *Village Voice*, 10–16 March 1999.

Smith, Roberta. "As You Live and Breathe, With, Um, a Couple of Adjustments." *New York Times*, 8 February 2002, E38.

Bruce Nauman

Selected Exhibitions

Solo

2002   Sperone Westwater Gallery, New York

1999   Donald Young Gallery, Chicago

1997   *Bruce Nauman, Image/Text 1966–1996*, Kunstmuseum Wolfsburg, Wolfsburg, Germany

        Bruce Nauman: 1985–1996, Drawings, Prints, and Related Works, Aldrich Museum of Contemporary Art, Ridgefield, Conn.

Group

2001   *Into the Light: The Projected Image in American Art 1964–1977*, Whitney Museum of American Art, New York

2000   *Crossroads of American Sculpture*, Indianapolis Museum of Art

1998   *Surrogate: The Figure in Contemporary Sculpture and Photography*, Henry Art Gallery, Seattle, Wash.

Selected Bibliography

Benezra, Neal, Kathy Halbreich, Robert Storr et al. *Bruce Nauman*. Minneapolis: Walker Art Center, 1994.

Kimmelman, Michael. "Art in Review: Bruce Nauman—'Mapping the Studio I & II (Fat Chance John Cage).'" *New York Times*, 5 July 2002, E35.

Morgan, Robert C., ed. *Bruce Nauman*. Baltimore: The Johns Hopkins University Press, 2002.

Nauman, Bruce. "Bruce Nauman Talks About *Mapping the Studio*." *Artforum* 40 (March 2002): 120–21.

Saltz, Jerry. "Wild Kingdom." *Village Voice*, 5 February 2002, 57.

Schjeldahl, Peter. "Night Moves: The indifferent grandeur of Bruce Nauman." *The New Yorker*, 28 January 2002, 94–95.

Simon, Joan, general editor, with Janet Jenkins and Toby Kamps. *Bruce Nauman: Exhibition Catalogue and Catalogue Raisonné*. Minneapolis: Walker Art Center, 1994.

Wei, Lilly. "Bruce Nauman at Dia." *Art in America* (June 2002): 120.

Nigel Poor

Selected Exhibitions

Solo

2002   Haines Gallery, San Francisco

2000   Haines Gallery, San Francisco

1996   *Between the Elements: Photographs by Nigel Poor*, Sol
Mednick Gallery, University of the Arts, Philadelphia

Group

2000   *Beyond Boundaries: Contemporary Photography in California*,
The Friends of Photography, San Francisco

1999   *Current Works 99*, Society for Contemporary Photography,
Kansas City, Mo.

1997   *Illuminance*, Fine Arts Center, Lubbock, Texas

Vision Gallery, Chandler Center for the Arts, Chandler, Ariz.

1996   *This is a Set Up: Fab Photo/Fictions*, Fine Arts Center Galleries,
Bowling Green State University, Bowling Green, Ohio

Selected Bibliography

Elliot Sherman, Ann. "Poor's Rich Photos." *Metro*, vol. 13,
10–16 April 1997, 35.

Kabat, Nora. *Beyond Boundaries: Contemporary Photography
in California*. San Francisco: The Friends of Photography, 2000.

Susan Smith-Pinelo

Selected Exhibitions

Solo

2002   Fusebox, Washington, D.C.

Patricia Faure Gallery, Santa Monica, Calif.

Group

2002   *Shoot the Singer: Music on Video*, Institute of Contemporary Art, University of Pennsylvania, Philadelphia

2001   *Race in Digital Space*, List Visual Arts Center, Massachusetts Institute of Technology, Cambridge, Mass.

One Planet Under A Groove: Hip Hop and Contemporary Art, Bronx Museum, New York

Freestyle, Studio Museum in Harlem, New York

Altoids Curiously Strong Collection, New Museum of Contemporary Art, New York

1998   12ᵗʰ Annual Washington International Film Festival, Kennedy Center, Washington, D.C.

School 33 Arts Center, Baltimore

ARTSITES 98, WPA/Corcoran Project Space, Washington, D.C.

Selected Bibliography

Cotter, Holland. "Beyond Multiculturalism, Freedom?" *New York Times*, 29 July 2001, section 2, p. 1.

Golden, Thelma. *Freestyle*. New York: Studio Museum in Harlem, 2001.

Plagens, Peter. "Harlem Goes 'Freestyle.'" *Newsweek*, 14 May 2001, 60.

Saltz, Jerry. "Post-Black." *Village Voice*, 22 May 2001, 51–52.

Schjeldahl, Peter. "Breaking Away." *The New Yorker*, 11 June 2001, 90–91.

Valdez, Sarah. "Freestyling." *Art in America* (September 2001): 134–39, 162.

Wiltz, Teresa. "Art and the Body Politic, Susan Smith-Pinelo Lays Bare Issues of Female Identity." *Washington Post*, 12 December 2001, C1.

Bruce Yonemoto

Selected Exhibitions

Solo

2001   *Bruce Yonemoto: Screen Gems*, Kemper Museum of Contemporary Art, Kansas City, Mo.

The Time Machine, Blum & Poe, Santa Monica, Calif.

Bruce Yonemoto, Institute of Contemporary Art, University of Pennsylvania, Philadelphia

1999   *Bruce Yonemoto: Disappearance of Memory*, NTT Intercommunication Center, Tokyo

Bruce and Norman Yonemoto: Memory Matter and Modern Romance, Japanese American National Museum, Los Angeles

Group

2000   *Made in California: Art, Image & Identity, 1900–2000*, Los Angeles County Museum of Art

Video Time, Museum of Modern Art, New York

Tempis Fugit, Nelson-Atkins Museum, Kansas City, Mo.

1997   *American Stories: Amidst Displacement and Transformation*, Setagaya Art Museum, Tokyo

Selected Bibliography

Klonarides, Carole Ann, Takuo Komatsuzaki, and Bruce Yonemoto. *Bruce Yonemoto: Disappearance of Memory*. Tokyo: NTT Intercommunication Center, 1999.

Ollman, Leah. "Bruce and Norman Yonemoto at the Japanese American National Museum." *Art in America* (September 1999): 134.

Buruma, Ian, Karin Higa, and Timothy Martin. *Bruce and Norman Yonemoto: Memory Matter and Modern Romance*. Los Angeles: Japanese American National Museum, 1999.

Knight, Christopher. "Insightful, Social Special Effects." *Los Angeles Times*, 24 January 1999, 6, 69.

Checklist

Linda Besemer

Fold #54, 2001
Acrylic paint over aluminum rod
32 x 76 1/8 x 2"
Collection of Mr. and Mrs. Frank Herringer

Fold #55, 2001
Acrylic paint over aluminum rod
72 x 80 ⁻/8 x 2"
Courtesy the artist and Angles Gallery, Santa
Monica, Calif.

Fold #56, 2001
Acrylic paint over aluminum rod
31 1/2 x 76 3/8 x 2"
Collection of Curtis Liberda and
Chris Esworthy, Dallas

Fold Quadrant #5, 2001
Acrylic paint over aluminum rod
73 x 80 1/8 x 2"
Collection of Phyllis and John Kleinberg

Janet Cardiff and George Bures Miller

The Paradise Institute, 2001
Wood, theater seats, DVD, DVD player, digital
projector, headphones, and mixed media
Edition of 5 with 1 artist's proof
120 x 449 x 201"
Courtesy Luhring Augustine, New York, and Galerie
Barbara Weiss, Berlin

Nancy Davidson

Double Exposure, 2002
Vinyl-coated nylon, tethers, rope, electrical wires,
400-watt metal halide light, and blower
240 x 240 x 408"
Courtesy the artist and Robert Miller Gallery, New
York. Commissioned by the Corcoran Gallery of Art

Marcel Dzama

174 untitled drawings, 2000, 2001, and 2002
Varying combinations of gouache, watercolor, root-
beer base, ink, and pencil on paper
Each 14 x 11"
Courtesy the artist and David Zwirner, New York

Jacob El Hanani

Weavings, 1982
Ink on paper
19 x 19"
Collection of the artist

Alef-Beth, 1992
Ink on paper
18 3/4 x 18 5/8"
Collection of Nicole Klagsbrun, New York

Ketuvim, 1995
Ink on paper
10 x 7 1/2"
Collection of Leslie Camhi, New York

Jacob El Hanani (from the "Signature" series),
1996
Ink on paper
19 x 19"
Courtesy Gallery Joe, Philadelphia

NOF–98, 1998
Ink on paper
19 x 19"
Private Collection, New York, Courtesy Nicole
Klagsbrun Gallery, New York

Script, 1998
Ink on paper
19 x 19"
Courtesy Nicole Klagsbrun Gallery, New York

Alef-Beth-99-2000, 1999–2000
Ink on paper
22 1/2 x 28 1/2"
Courtesy Nicole Klagsbrun Gallery, New York

Dish Towel Grid, 2000
Ink on paper
6 x 12"
Courtesy Nicole Klagsbrun Gallery, New York

Alef-Beth Grid, 2001
Ink on paper
7 1/2 x 9 3/4"
Courtesy Nicole Klagsbrun Gallery, New York

Gauze, 2001
Ink on paper
23 1/2 x 37 1/2"
Courtesy Nicole Klagsbrun Gallery, New York

Landscape, 2002
Ink on paper
32 1/8 x 40 1/16"
Courtesy Nicole Klagsbrun Gallery, New York

Basket (from the "Basket" series), 2002
Ink on paper
32 1/8 x 40 1/16"
Courtesy Nicole Klagsbrun Gallery, New York

Ken Feingold

If/Then, 2001
Silicone, pigments, fiberglass, steel, electronics,
cardboard, and mixed media
24 x 24 x 28"
Collection of Anne Hoger and Robert Conn,
Del Mar, Calif.

Self Portrait as the Center of the Universe, 2001
Silicone, pigments, fiberglass, steel, electronics,
wood, ventriloquist puppets, digital projection, and
mixed media
68 x 36 x 36", installation dimensions with projection variable
Courtesy Postmasters Gallery, New York

Sinking Feeling, 2001
Silicone, pigments, fiberglass, steel, electronics,
wood, digital projection, and mixed media
52 x 15 x 18", installation dimensions with projection variable
Courtesy Postmasters Gallery, New York

Kojo Griffin

Untitled, 2001
Charcoal on paper
22 x 25 1/8"
Private Collection, Courtesy Mitchell-Innes &
Nash, New York

Untitled, 2001
Charcoal on paper
22 x 26 1/8"
Courtesy Mitchell-Innes & Nash, New York

Untitled (man handing candy to girl), 2001
Acrylic, collage, charcoal, and graphite on
wood panel
95 3/4 x 119 5/8"
Private Collection

Untitled (man with letter, woman standing), 2001
Acrylic, collage, charcoal, and graphite on paper
23 3/4 x 20 1/8"
Private Collection, Courtesy Mitchell-Innes &
Nash, New York

Untitled, 2002
Charcoal on paper
22 1/2 x 25 1/4"
Courtesy Saltworks Gallery, Atlanta

Untitled, 2002
Charcoal on paper
20 x 22 1/2"
Courtesy Saltworks Gallery, Atlanta

*Untitled (man helpin' man up, man walking
toward)*, 2002
Acrylic, collage, charcoal, and graphite on
wood panel
71 7/8 x 88 7/8"
P. Bruce Marine and Donald Hardy Collection

Untitled (man with girl), 2002
Acrylic, collage, charcoal, and graphite on
wood panel
48 x 60"
Partial and promised gift of P. Bruce Marine
and Donald Hardy

Tim Hawkinson

Drip, 2002
Polyethylene, vinyl, aluminum, mechanical com-
ponents, and water
10 x 12 x 15', installation dimensions variable
Courtesy the artist and Ace Gallery, Los Angeles
Commissioned by the Corcoran Gallery of Art

Bruce Nauman

*Mapping the Studio II with color shift, flip, flop &
flip/flop (Fat Chance John Cage) All Action Edit*,
2001
7 DVDs, 7 DVD players, 7 digital projectors,
7 pairs of speakers
10 x 12' images, installation dimensions variable
Collection Walker Art Center, Minneapolis, T. B.
Walker Acquisition Fund, 2002

Nigel Poor

Three Objects, 2002
216 C-prints
Sizes ranging from 11 x 11" to 5 1/2 x 5 1/2"
Courtesy the artist and Haines Gallery, San
Francisco, with the support of the Coastal Studies
Center, Bowdoin College, Brunswick, Maine.

Susan Smith-Pinelo

Dances with Hip Hop, 2000
3 DVDs, 3 DVD players, and 3 monitors
Installation dimensions variable
Courtesy Fusebox, Washington, D.C.

Asstronomical Proportions I (from the *Hiphopcrisy*
series), 2002
1 DVD, 1 DVD player, and 3 monitors
Installation dimensions variable
Courtesy Fusebox, Washington, D.C.

Asstronomical Proportions II (from the
Hiphopcrisy series), 2002
1 DVD, 1 DVD player, and 3 monitors
Installation dimensions variable
Courtesy Fusebox, Washington, D.C.

Bruce Yonemoto

Journey to the Center of the Earth, 2001
Globe, DVD player, 2.2" monitor, electrical cord,
and monocle
16 x 12 x 12"
Courtesy Blum & Poe, Santa Monica, Calif.

The Time Machine, 2001
Globe, DVD player, 2.2" monitor, electrical cord,
and monocle
16 x 12 x 12"
Courtesy Blum & Poe, Santa Monica, Calif.

Atlas, 2002
C-print
60 x 40"
Courtesy Blum & Poe, Santa Monica, Calif., and
lemon sky: projects + editions, Los Angeles

Dear Playboy, 2002
C-print
60 x 40"
Courtesy Blum & Poe, Santa Monica, Calif., and
lemon sky: projects + editions, Los Angeles

It's a Small World After All, 2002
Globe, stucco, CD player, audio amplifier, audio
speaker, and speaker wire
16 x 12 x 12"
Courtesy Blum & Poe, Santa Monica, Calif.

Panpanorama, 2002
DVD and DVD projector
12 x 16' image size, installation
dimensions variable
Courtesy Blum & Poe, Santa Monica, Calif.

Playboy After Hours, 2002
C-print
60 x 40"
Courtesy Blum & Poe, Santa Monica, Calif., and
lemon sky: projects + editions, Los Angeles

Spaceship Earth, 2002
Globe, DVD player, 2.2" monitor, electrical cord,
monocle, and headphones
14 x 11 x 11"
Courtesy Blum & Poe, Santa Monica, Calif.

*The Equator Is an Imaginary Line Around the
Earth*, 2002
Globe
16 x 12 x 12"
Courtesy Blum & Poe, Santa Monica, Calif.

The Playboy Advisor, 2002
C-print
60 x 40"
Courtesy Blum & Poe, Santa Monica, Calif., and
lemon sky: projects + editions, Los Angeles

Top of the World, 2002
Bar, globes, liquor bottles, electric lights, and
mixed media
50 x 139 x 104", installation dimensions variable
Courtesy Blum & Poe, Santa Monica, Calif.

About the Authors

Jonathan P. Binstock is curator of contemporary art at the Corcoran Gallery of Art and the organizer of many exhibitions, including *Andy Warhol: Social Observer* and *Primary Properties: Mary Judge, Joseph Dumbacher John Dumbacher.* He is currently working on a retrospective exhibition of the paintings of Sam Gilliam.

Matthew Biro is associate professor of modern and contemporary art and director of graduate studies in the Department of the History of Art at the University of Michigan, Ann Arbor. His book *Anselm Kiefer and the Philosophy of Martin Heidegger* was published by Cambridge University Press in 1998. His articles and reviews have appeared in *RES, Clio, New German Critique, Art Criticism*, and *New Art Examiner.* He is currently working on a book on cyborgs in Weimar culture.

Billy Collins is the poet laureate of the United States for 2001–2003 and has published seven collections of poetry, including *Nine Horses, Picnic Lightning, The Art of Drowning, Questions about Angels*, and *Sailing Alone Around the Room,* a compilation of his work. He is a Distinguished Professor of English at Lehman College of the City University of New York and a visiting writer at Sarah Lawrence College.

Adam Lerner, formerly the curator of the Contemporary Museum in Baltimore, is master teacher of modern and contemporary art at the Denver Art Museum. He has a Ph.D. from the Johns Hopkins University, where he wrote a dissertation examining public monuments and political action in early-twentieth-century America.

Stacey Schmidt is assistant curator of contemporary art at the Corcoran Gallery of Art and also works extensively with the Corcoran's collection of prints and drawings. She is the organizer of the exhibitions *William Newman: Peripheral Vision* and *Fashioning Art: Handbags by Judith Leiber.*

Jacquelyn Days Serwer is chief curator at the Corcoran Gallery of Art, where she oversees all museum activities. Her own work has focused on American and contemporary art. Most recently, she organized a retrospective exhibition of the work of Larry Rivers and contributed an essay to the accompanying book, *Larry Rivers: Art and the Artist*, published by Bulfinch Press.

Photograph Credits